An Introduction to English Language Teaching

82:96

D1395638

Longman Handbooks for Language Teachers

Longman Handbooks for Language Teachers
General Editor: Donn Byrne

An Introduction to English Language Teaching

REVISED IMPRESSION

John Haycraft

Longman

Longman Group UK Limited,
Longman House, Burnt Mill, Harlow,
Essex CM20 2JE England
and Associated Companies throughout the world

© Longman Group Ltd. 1978

First published 1978
Revised impression 1986
Fifteenth impression 1992

ISBN 0-582-55604-X

Produced by Longman Singapore Publishers Pte Ltd
Printed in Singapore

Purpose

This book is designed for those who know little or nothing about teaching English as a foreign or second language. It is, therefore, suitable pre-course reading for an RSA Preparatory Certificate, or any other form of initial training. Conspicuous for its lack of jargon, and minimal philosophic theory, it provides a basic outline of many of the practical approaches and techniques which need to be applied in the classroom. Describing such things is a little like trying to explain how to play tennis or how to sing an aria. When using this book, therefore, try to visualise everything in action. Remember, too, that a summary of this sort can, normally, only suggest one or two ways of dealing with a problem. There are, for instance, many ways of developing a mime story or teaching through picture composition. Everything will also depend on another variable: the kind of students you are teaching.

Everything in this book has been taught in one form or another on International House teachers' courses. This does not mean, however, that all our courses follow precisely what is contained in the following pages. Although basic assumptions probably remain remarkably consistent in the field of English as a foreign language, new ideas may arise continually, and the personality of each teacher trainer also determines the development of the course.

Because the most unfamiliar problem for new teachers is communication with those who speak little English, the book deals mainly with the stage from Beginners to Intermediate, and concentrates principally on the oral approach.

I would like to thank all those who have contributed directly or indirectly to this book through classrooms all over the world: particularly my wife, Brita Haycraft, for much of what is contained in the section on Pronunciation; Jean Stokes for her summary of ideas on vocabulary teaching; Lyn Williams for classifying oral drills; Doug Case for his work on flash cards; Joan Holby and Helen Moorwood for their ideas on mime; Ken Wilson's songs on teaching; Alan Wakeman, Anwi Buckingham and Sheila Sullivan for their work on the language laboratory; Felicity Henderson and Tim Lowe for the bibliographies; John Meredith Parry for his comments on projectors and exams; Brian Nevitt for his work on video, Judy Lugton for her outline of Selected Readers, Angela Cleverley and Martin Parrott for their editorial work.

Finally, I should like to thank the successive directors of the Institute whose one idea has been to improve the quality and professionalism of teacher training: Roger Gannon, David Dickinson, Lin Hutton, Lyn Williams, Derek Hooper, Georgie Raman, Liz Baines and Tony Duff.

JH

iii

Contents

To Katinka

Introduction – foreigner to foreigner

Teaching and learning a language inevitably involve relationships between different nationalities. A study of the possible intricacies of the relationships would fill a book. However, it is worth trying here to examine some of the underlying factors which can affect both the learner and the teacher of English. English teachers often work abroad and many students of English study in English speaking countries. In addition, language is the unique expression of an NB/ historical development, of a special social awareness, and of particular ways of thought. Learning and teaching it will necessarily involve adapting to the culture and attitudes of which it is an essential facet.

One point to be remembered is that we are all in some way nationalistic – 'provincial' and chauvinistic at heart, however rational we believe we are. Again, most of us are influenced more by what happens to us personally, than by seemingly objective judgements. People often like or dislike a country because the visit was the occasion of a successful or unsuccessful love affair or business venture, or because they have met a few people from the country who have been good friends or surly enemies.

However, where this goes wrong is when we relate the personal reaction to the 'objective' judgment. This is probably at the root of most of the problems of foreigner to foreigner and can lead to various difficulties.

Living abroad

A foreigner has great advantages. He is classless. He is often welcomed simply because he comes from another country. People want to impress him, and he also has the distinction of being exotic and different – except in areas where there are more tourists or immigrants than local inhabitants. The foreigner also has the advantage of being able to find easy subjects for conversation: people question him about his country and tell about theirs, and he will usually find a ready bond with people who have visited his country – whether they are eulogistic or critical.

Apart from this, he usually has the advantage of a stimulating environment because everything is new, and even the most commonplace social habits are interesting because they are different. He is excused if he occasionally ignores everyday conventions because he is not expected to be familiar with them, and in this way he has more latitude than he has at home. Because he is a foreigner, he is expected to be helpless and therefore will receive more kindness. At the same time, he is not committed. Other people's revolutions, poverty, or wars may interest him, but they rarely threaten him directly. If he gets exasperated, he can escape, as long as he has enough money for a ticket home.

1

On the other hand, those in the community around him have their own friends, relatives and loves. They know the way the community works. They are familiar with the assumptions and attitudes which guide relations between people. Even if he speaks the language quite well, the foreigner can rarely communicate really adequately, and expressing or understanding humour are usually beyond him. Even if he lives in another country for a time, he is still regarded as someone who is always different per se. As he gets to know the community better, he also becomes aware of the barriers which religion, politics, and 'tribal groupings' have erected. As he stays on, he may get bored with standard reactions to his foreign status, realise that there are also people who are prejudiced against him because of his nationality, and become aware that he really is an outsider. This can lead to:

The defensive syndrome

As a result of these feelings of isolation, the foreigner often reacts by creating his own defensive barriers. These make him feel better, but they do in fact isolate him further. To rehabilitate his self-confidence, he compares everything he sees unfavourably with what he imagines his own country to be like. Because he does not speak or understand the language well enough, he feels conversation and humour are not nearly so stimulating as in his own circles at home. Because he cannot understand books or plays, he presumes his own literature is superior. If he feels he has not been welcomed sufficiently, he asserts that people in his own country welcome foreigners much more warmly – largely because he can only remember the times when foreigners were welcomed, and knows nothing of when they were not. He also begins to patronise and criticise the country he is in, and then blames those who object to this. He talks of the need for accepting criticism, while forgetting that he would probably not take very warmly to that kind of criticism from foreigners at home. Whenever an individual does something which displeases him, he brands the action as typical of the whole country. He may end up isolating himself in a little group of his own countrymen who also suffer from the same symptoms of aggressive self-pity, and together they reinforce their own defensive prejudices by establishing their own way of life wherever they go.

Fortunately, there are not many foreigners who suffer all the extreme forms of this disease. Symptoms, however, occur with all of us, and only if we are aware of their origin can we prevent the scratches from developing into blood poisoning. For the tourist, probably, or for the itinerant business man, this whole question does not matter much anyway, as they are not really involved in the country they are visiting. However, for those who really want to teach, or learn a language abroad, the 'defensive syndrome' can be crippling.

The generalisation syndrome

Generalisations are a useful rule of thumb which can help the traveller to clarify his impressions. They can be valid. That Mediterranean peoples entertain less in their homes than English people, that Spanish families are more closely knit than

English ones, or that people have less time to speak to strangers in London than in a Calabrian village, are statements that are generally true.

However, where generalisations go wrong is when they cease to be stages of thought and become immutable rules or prejudices, where exceptions are not allowed, or somehow twisted to conform to the rule. When a student arrives in England with the fixed idea that all Englishmen are cold and reserved, he does himself harm, because, as a result, he does not try to make English friends. Again, a visitor to Africa who believes everything is dirty and unhygienic becomes a 'greenhouse traveller', unable to penetrate beyond the confines of international hotels.

It is of course impossible to find generalisations which apply accurately to millions of people, spread over different counties or provinces, which themselves differ in custom or outlook and often in race. Many generalisations spring from ancient hearsay: to some people who have never been in England, the bowler hat and the pea-soup fog still reign supreme. Again, Spaniards are often regarded as cruel because of the Civil War which ended years ago – or even because of the Inquisition, which was abolished in 1804.

Newspapers and television convey as many false impressions as true ones because they tend to focus on other countries mainly when there is a crisis or some disaster, and most roving reporters do not speak the language of the country.

Many people get their ideas of other countries from an older generation of parents or teachers, or from history books which are usually full of nationalistic distortions.

Many generalisations are part of the 'defensive syndrome' and consist of comparative value judgements which are bound to be invalid. It is possible, for example, to say that there are more cars per head of population in Britain than Algeria, but that does not mean that Britain is 'superior' in any way. The number of cars on the roads is merely one facet of two very different and complex ways of life. Very often, comparing countries in superior or inferior terms is as absurd as stating that a tree is 'better' per se than a stone, or vice-versa. In fact, what is interesting about a tree and a stone, or most national characteristics, is simply that they are different.

Thus generalisations can be of help as stages of thought, clarifying and defining so that they can then be challenged and remoulded by new impressions, new information, and the re-definition of terms. However, generalisations can become like the shell on the back of a slow-moving tortoise. Then the foreigner is as accurate about his view of the outside world as if he thought the earth was flat.

The intolerance syndrome

Intolerance is sometimes regarded as a necessary concomitant of conviction or faith, and tolerance as a form of flabby indifference. Obviously, many things are intolerable and, at the same time, there is no reason why an individual should be tolerant of what he feels is tyranny, mindless exploitations, or any other kind of infamy.

At the same time, intolerance can be the result of prejudice, ignorance of

essential facts, and of a failure to understand why another country has
developed as it has.

This is where a knowledge of the history of other countries plays an important
role. If one knows the background and life-story of an individual, it is obviously
much easier to understand why he is what he is and why he does, or has done,
certain things. In the same way, it is difficult to understand much about France if
one knows nothing of Louis XIV, or the Revolution, or Napoleon, or 1940. It is
difficult to understand Spain without knowing something about the Catholic
Church, the expulsion of the Moors, the colonisation of South America, or the
causes of the Civil War. Because everything changes so rapidly today, history is
often regarded as the study of the remote: the examination of dead things. In
fact, though, as Acton said, the causes of the American War of Independence
can be found in the forests of Germany – just as many contemporary phenomena
of Italy can be traced back to the foreign invasions of the sixteenth century, or
elements in present day England can be linked to the Norman Conquest, or
Cromwell's Major-Generals. Today, also, we tend to discount religious
differences, yet one of the things that makes English ways of thought so different
from that of our neighbours is the fact that the 'Establishment' has been affected
by Anglican rather than by Catholic or Protestant assumptions.

Apart from this, tolerance is possible only if certain premises are accepted.
The first is that all members of religions other than one's own are not damned
to perdition. The second is the admission that different political forms may suit
different countries at different stages of their development. And the third is that
every citizen is not wholly responsible for the wrongs committed by his
government. Ironically, teaching languages under reactionary regimes is more
necessary because it often represents the students' only real contact with other
countries. Again, bias against a student because he belongs to a country whose
regime one dislikes, or has religious beliefs one disapproves of, is not only
unjustifiable, but is also to teach him less well.

Tolerance as far as foreigners are concerned does not, then, mean adopting an
apathetic view of the universe where all personal convictions give way to the
feeling that disapproval is taboo. It simply means being less intolerant of things
one knows very little about, being wary of propaganda, and trying to find out,
not only through language but also through the history and geography of a
country, why people think and act differently.

The teacher's opportunity

Shouldn't it be possible to go to another country simply for the sun, for better
food, because there are friends of one's own nationality there whom one likes,
because living is cheaper, or simply because, assailed by restlessness, one needs a
change? Surely it would be intolerable if countries were overrun by earnest
foreigners all trying to integrate, and avoid heretical thoughts.

Again, can't one get the most out of a country, simply by being interested in
people, without having to delve into their past or politics? And as an English
teacher abroad, why learn the language? Some believe they are incapable of it, or

that they can 'pick up' enough, or that they can get around with English anyway, or mime.

Obviously, everyone should work out their own approach abroad, according to their interests and their own personality. Nevertheless, it would be foolish to become an actor if one was not interested in the theatre, a novelist if one was bored with literature, or a concert pianist if one was not fascinated by music. In the same way, it is probably misguided to become a teacher of English as a foreign language if one is not interested in learning languages and exploring the countries from which one's students come.

The English teacher, after all, has a unique opportunity to get to know other countries. A business man abroad is usually limited to narrow circles of colleagues. A tourist gets to know the sights, the beaches, and the night clubs. An English teacher, however, with perhaps half a dozen classes coming for three hours a week, will probably know over a hundred students very well within a few months. These students usually come from every walk of life, talk about themselves in class, encourage their teacher to learn their language, and help him/her to get to know their country. At home, the English teacher will meet students from all over the world. If English is not his mother tongue, he/she will get to know the English and the Anglo-Saxon world much better through teaching. The English teacher then, has unlimited possibilities for becoming 'international'.

1 Some basic principles

Teaching English successfully is not just a question of method. I have observed classes where the teacher's techniques were superb, but where the students were reluctant to learn because the teacher was not interested in them as people, and his lesson developed like the workings of a machine, functioning in isolation. Techniques are there to be varied according to who, and what, is being taught.

The world of English teaching is as full of dogmatic sects as seventeenth century England. Prophets arise and new denominations are formed which believe that a 'structural', a 'notional', or 'a communicative approach' is the only path to a promised land where all students speak perfect English and pass their exams without difficulty. Many of these ideas may be valid in their own way, but they are not exclusive.

Language would seem to reflect life, and perhaps teaching English should, therefore, be as varied as living, and include as many approaches as possible. However, just as the teaching of English is poorer when informed by a single idea, so it is of doubtful effectiveness if it is anarchic, with amateurs 'doing their thing' and students learning, or not learning, through osmosis.

Every teacher develops his own method over a period of time. He tries out different techniques and refines those that suit him and the subject matter he is dealing with. This book, therefore, attempts to outline various techniques that can form part of the teacher's 'armoury'.

Underlying English teaching, whether to adults or children, whether in Norway or Papua, there are probably a number of obvious, commonsense, practical assumptions, as well as an awareness of learning processes and of how language works as a medium of communication.

1.1. The student – involving the student and maintaining interest

Students should look forward to their English lessons and be sorry when they are over. They should work hard because they are interested. Given this, the following considerations can be borne in mind:

1.1.1. The importance of motivation

Motivation can be summed up, briefly, as the student's desire and need to learn – the driving force that makes him work hard, pay attention, and so on. The teacher's own determination that the students should learn is an important contribution to this, as is encouragement and a sense of progress which should also come from the teacher.

6

1.1.2. The problem of psychological resistance

It is our job to make sure that our students are at ease. If they are learning outside their own country, it is important that they feel welcome, well looked-after, and comfortable. We need to discover the 'blocks' which a student has when learning English: perhaps a teacher once told him he was incapable of learning; perhaps his family dislikes the British or Americans; perhaps he feels overawed by the other students, or thinks the teacher dislikes him. There can be hundreds of other barriers to learning and, ideally, every school needs its language psychiatrist. However, as the profession has yet to be invented, we, as teachers, are responsible for finding out about our students, relaxing them, and convincing them that their fears about learning English are illusory.

1.1.3. The need for personalisation

Students involve themselves when a lesson allows them to talk about themselves or what is closest to them. It is necessary, therefore, to get to know our students' interests and backgrounds. If the class is fascinated by football, it is as well to use it in examples and situations. If an English teacher is employed in Bangkok or Rome, he should get to know these cities, so that he can ask relevant questions and get his students to express their own experiences in English. The ideal teaching situation is achieved when all the students are bursting to say something in English which interests them passionately. The language taught must be seen to be meaningful, useful, and manageable to them.

1.1.4. The need for realism

The nearer language teaching can come to real life, the more interesting it will be. Situations and realistic examples of language use which the students will meet outside the classroom should be used as much as possible. For the same reason, words, structure, and idiom should, preferably, be taught in a context.
Most people react more strongly to feelings than to abstractions. Part of teaching English realistically, therefore, is getting students to express moods and attitudes. It is easy to introduce contradiction or argument in English right at the beginning. Standard statements can be made more interesting by saying them impatiently, persuasively, enthusiastically, sweetly, amazedly, scornfully. You may find yourself using uninteresting questions and answers to practise a particular point, e.g. 'What's the colour of your shirt?' 'It's green'. This is a fairly unreal exchange at the best of times. If, however, the answer is made in a deprecating tone with 'of course' at the end, you automatically make it more acceptable. The expression of attitudes and feelings can be the life-blood of a class.

1.1.5. The need to give confidence – acting out

Performing short sketches and dialogues involves students in a special way, whether as interested listeners or as active participants. The concentration on movement, character and mime makes a student less self-conscious about what he is actually saying. The nervous effort involved, once conquered, also assures the student that he need not be frightened of speaking English. Thus often if he can ask the way in English in a sketch in front of a whole class, he feels more confident about doing it in real life. Acting out can also be used as a prelude to improvisation, which is what students will have to do constantly, once they speak the language.

1.1.6. The need to maintain interest – pace and variety

A class should progress as rapidly as it is able to. You will only know how fast your students can go by experimenting with different tempos. Many classes are dominated by the teacher and, as a result, the students' potential is rarely used to the full, and impatience rather than enthusiasm is generated. At the same time we have to alternate intense work with relaxation, following a concentrated listening comprehension, say, with games or a song.

Monotony produces sleepiness and it is essential, therefore, to use as many different activities as possible, even when teaching the same language item. You could, for instance, concentrate on the same point for three hours on end, as long as you used a new activity every half hour. For instance, if your main aim was to teach some of the differences between *some* and *any*, you could use the following activities: 1. question and answer in a situation; 2. a taped dialogue; 3. a passage read for comprehension; 4. a dictation; 5. acting out a scene in a shop; 6. describing objects. Even after three hours, the students would probably have a sense of variety, and a feeling of satisfaction at having achieved a lot. In addition, a large number of other things would have been practised, along with familiarisation of this point.

1.2. The language

To be able to use language to convey thoughts/intentions/wishes/information etc. a person needs a mastery of various elements.

The individual *sounds*, which are arranged in *words* (the vocabulary, or lexis, of the language), which are related to each other in utterances by *structure* (the grammer of a language). For example, 'He can swim well.' and 'Can he swim well?' use the same words – but from the different relationships of the words to each other, we understand that the first is a statement of fact and the second is a question, seeking to establish a fact of which we are unsure. The different aspects of *pronunciation* – stress and intonation – can also give a different significance to an utterance. In respect of written language, the *written symbols* that represent the spoken word are also involved.

Then there are various *skills* involved in the mastery of a language: *receptive* skills, listening (understanding the spoken language) and reading (understanding the written language); and *productive* skills – speaking and writing. These involve a further element, *selection* of the relevant language for the situation concerned.

Having looked at these various elements of language, we need to examine the implications from the point of view of course content.

1.3. Course content

1.3.1. Skills

Before we decide what kind of practice our class needs, we have to know why our students are learning English and what they want it for. Is it for passing an exam, writing business reports, working as telephone operators, understanding medical journals, talking to tourists? Within the main linguistic skills mentioned above there are scores of secondary skills (see 3.1.1.). Understanding a person speaking directly to you in a foreign language is different from trying to make out what two people talking together are saying. Different again are telephone conversations, plays, films, radio broadcasts. When planning a syllabus, you therefore have to consider not only structure, vocabulary, and idiom, but also how your students will be using these and why.

1.3.2. Structure

There are many different attitudes towards the teaching of grammar. There are doubts about whether it should be taught explicitly at all, whether the selection of structures to teach should be based on simplicity, leading to a carefully graded sequence of increasing difficulty, or whether selection should be on the grounds of frequency of occurrence in the language, or usefulness to the pupil. Whatever the theory, the fact remains that there are patterns in English that the student needs to master. Most nationalities are more conditioned to the grammatical analysis of their own language than we are. Often, therefore, they may feel more at ease if given rules first (for example: to form the plural in English we normally add an 's', but there are certain exceptions). Rules however will usually disappear, like scaffolding round a new building, when you have given enough practice to allow your students to think directly in English rather than analytically. Much of English cannot, in any case, be fitted into rules. However, where it can, the student does have the advantage of knowing formulae which he can apply to new language situations. In general, it is probably better to get your class to elicit the rules from the language you are teaching, as you are thus making them think for themselves – i.e. you present them with examples of the point you wish to teach and the formulation of rules follows from that. Certainly, it is essential for you, yourself, to know as much as possible about English grammar – as seen from the linguistic angle of the students you are teaching (see Chapter 4).

1.3.3. Vocabulary

General principles for the selection of vocabulary when teaching English are considered in detail in Chapter 5.

1.3.4. Phrases, idioms and colloquial usages

A lot of English can be taught and learned simply because it is appropriate to the teaching situation: 'Good morning/afternoon', 'very good', 'not bad', 'repeat', 'all together', 'see you tomorrow' etc. It is often worth teaching other useful expressions in their context before getting on to analysing their structure: 'I don't know/understand/agree', 'What does this mean?', 'What's your job?' etc.

1.3.5. Pronunciation

Teachers are often reluctant to teach this methodically, but it is as essential to speaking as spelling is to writing. An utterance can have a score of different meanings depending on the intonation – for example, 'Yes' said in different ways can convey: simple agreement, surprise, doubt, enquiry, etc. Contrary to popular belief, it is possible to find a number of guidelines for teaching pronunciation (see Chapter 6). Ideally, it should be integrated with other forms of teaching. Recent research indicates that it is often what students are most anxious to perfect when learning English. It also gives an essential element of realism to any class and brings 'dead' sentences and situations alive.

1.4. Teaching sequence for introducing new language items

1.4.1. Selection

The amount of material introduced should be such that students can learn to use it quickly and easily. A beginner, learning to ski, uses small, light skis initially, and only when he has learnt to manoeuvre on these, does he put on normal, heavy skis. In the same way, few students can learn to use forty new words, or three new structures, in an hour. A mass of material like this will make them feel helpless. Make sure therefore that your students can use what you have taught them before you feed in more. Or else, introduce something new, briefly, then revise something you have already taught, revise what you have just introduced; then practise this new material blended with the English your students already know. If your class can use structure and idiom with ease they will accumulate the vocabulary they need as they find themselves in different situations.

1.4.2. Presentation and explanation

New material should be presented efficiently and effectively – in such a way as to make the meaning as clear and as memorable as possible.

1.4.2.1. SPEECH BEFORE WRITING

Because English pronunciation is different from its written form and inconsistent (e.g. *though, thought, cough, bough*), it is advisable to introduce and consolidate new material orally and only write up new words when your students can pronounce them. Otherwise there will be continual mother tongue interference and students will tend to pronounce English as if it were written in their own language. With passive vocabulary other considerations are important. (See section 5.4)

1.4.2.2. REPETITION

The easiest way, initially, of making students familiar with new words and phrases is through careful listening followed by repetition. This can be a dull exercise and should therefore be enlivened with variety and an imaginative approach. It is doubtful if any of the drills used should last more than a minute or so.

1.4.3. Practice

Most students need to learn how to use English rather than how to analyse it. They will do this best if they themselves practise the language they *need*. The teacher therefore should move on quickly from presentation to practice: at first controlled and guided practice, moving on to free activities (see Chapter 8).

1.4.4. Remedial work

This is an essential part of practice. As students progress they develop various problems – such as difficulty with prepositions or certain verb tenses. The teacher has to be aware of his individual students' problems and decide on a course of action to help remedy them. At intermediate or advanced stages, much of the teaching comes from setting compositions or projects, and then showing the students how to improve what they have said or written.

1.4.5. Revision of language

Teaching English can be like painting a wall. You put on one coat, then let it dry. Then you put on another coat and let it dry. Then you put on a third coat. It is usually best to let students 'sleep' on anything new. They will learn much better if reminded repeatedly over days, weeks, or even months, of language items that you have introduced. If you are excessively methodical and teach, say, nothing but the 'pluperfect' for three weeks and then go on to something else, your students may start using 'I had . . .' for all tenses in the past. They may then forget it when you absorb them in something new. Continual revision, and bringing in past lessons when introducing new ones, is essential.

1.5. Other considerations

1.5.1. The language the teacher uses

There are many points of view about whether students should learn British as opposed to American English and whether they should avoid regional accents. In general, an English teacher ought to teach the kind of English he himself speaks without self-consciousness, making sure, however, that he does not use purely 'local' colloquialisms. What is really important is that students are trained to understand different kinds of spoken English: American, British, Canadian – even French and German English. English, after all, is often used as a form of communication between non-English nationalities. Some pupils suffer from the problem of understanding only their teacher – this can be helped by the teacher bringing other forms of English into the classroom – most easily done on tape – to give students varied practice in listening.

Another consideration is that English is normally spoken reasonably fast, and from the beginning a student must accustom himself to this or he will be bewildered when he hears normal English spoken. At the same time, it is

incorrect to speak English without shortened forms (*he's*, *I'm*, *isn't*, etc).
Teachers often produce stilted English because they feel their students won't
understand otherwise. The result is that their classes speak like Daleks.

1.5.2.   The use of the student's mother tongue

If the teacher knows the student's mother tongue, translating individual words
can be a short cut to vocabulary teaching. However, a word is more likely to be
vivid, and thus better remembered, if taught in context, or associated with the
objects it represents. Again, a brief outline of a situation in the student's native
language can help set a context and aid rapid understanding of the items being
introduced.

Also, contrasting structural differences between English and the students'
own language can clarify a point. However, translating can also be a hindrance
to the learning process by discouraging the student from thinking in English,
and when sentences are translated directly from one language to another, a
lot of remedial teaching becomes necessary. Translation is itself a language
skill and should be practised at an advanced stage if a student is going to
be a translator or an interpreter. Otherwise it takes time away from the practice
of other skills which a student is more likely to need if he wants to speak
and write fluent English.

1.5.3.   The use of aids

Just as nothing should be taught unless it fulfills a need, or your aims, so aids
should be used as a means to an end, not an end in themselves. Too many
teachers regard their textbooks as a chaise longue on which they can relax, or as
a 'Bible' to be followed word for word. The language laboratory, too, is
something to be integrated into class work and not regarded as an object with
magical properties which deserves reverence. It is the teacher who teaches, but to
do this he must also know how to use visual aids and tapes, and all other
techniques of teaching. You should always ask yourself why you are choosing
certain aids and adapt them to your class and level – not just use them because
you think they have some intrinsic value of their own (see Chapter 10).

Further reading

1   On the students: Finocchiaro, M. and Bonomo N., *The Foreign Language
Learner*, Regents Publishing Co., 1973.

2   Byrne, D., *Teaching Oral English*, Longman, 1986. Chapters 1 and 2.

3   Littlewood, W., *Communicative Language Teaching*, CUP, 1983.

4   Holden, S. ed., *Visual Aids for Classroom Interaction*, MEP.

Discussion

1 Can you think of any other arguments to be made for and against the teaching of grammar in class?

2 What arguments for and against using translation as a means of learning a language can you think of?

3 What 'blocks' to language learning can you think of?

Exercises

1 If you are currently teaching a class, enumerate your students' main interests.

2 If you have taught English before, write down ways in which you were too 'dominating' as a teacher.

2 Some basic classroom techniques

The aim in any class is to involve all the students all the time. It is only too easy to waste time through imperfect techniques, and to find yourself giving a series of private classes, instead of teaching the group as a whole. Most students have a maximum of 90 hours of English throughout the year, and if you divide these up into a timetable, you will realise how little teaching time you have. Here are a few simple techniques which are not difficult to remember, but which few teachers manage to observe all the time:

Look at all the students in the class

The nervous teacher, starting a class, tends to find an area of friendly faces and to concentrate on them for comfort. However, those whom he does not look at will feel excluded, and may think that he dislikes them or that they are so insignificant that he is not even aware of them. When you are teaching, switch your gaze evenly from one side to another, like a well-regulated lighthouse. You will also have the advantage of knowing what is going on in the class the whole time, so that you are aware of who is paying attention and who isn't, and you can adapt your teaching accordingly.

Vary your techniques for asking questions

Questions are a way of compelling the attention of your students. If someone is yawning in the back row, ask him a question. However, don't start with the name of the student you are addressing: '*Pepe*, what was the name of Rebecca's husband?' Immediately you say 'Pepe', the rest of the class switch off, apart from their faint interest in what Pepe is going to say. Instead, say 'Who was Rebecca's husband?' Then pause and look round. Everyone, thinking they will be asked, will then work out the answer. When you finally name Pepe, the other students will be interested to know whether his answer is going to correspond with theirs.

Don't go round the class

It's better not to ask questions or to do exercises in rote around the class. Otherwise, those furthest away from the questioning know they can relax for some time before their turn comes, while those who have already answered can sit back and dream, knowing that they will probably not be asked again. Dart hither and thither and go back to someone you've just questioned, so that everyone realises he or she may be asked at any time.

Include everyone
Make sure that everyone is called on equally. Your own warmth and feeling for your students are a crucial basis for encouragement and motivation. It is only too easy, though, to 'forget' one's own students, particularly those that sit at the back, or on the 'wings' of the class.

Make sure the class is seated in the best possible way
It may be impossible to avoid having your students sitting in rows facing you. Even here, however, ensure that empty seats are only at the back and that everyone is grouped as near the front as possible. Ideally, everyone should be able to see everyone else, so that they can all participate in what is being said. Probably the best arrangement is to have everyone ranged round the wall, in a circle. You then get a large area in the middle which can be used for acting out, and there is a greater sense of community. If you are teaching with a wall-chart don't forget to bring everyone close to the place where you have hung it.

Limit teacher talking time
The more a teacher talks, the less will his students be given the opportunity of expressing themselves. Teaching English to foreigners is, therefore, not a suitable profession for someone who likes the sound of his own voice. A teacher, should, ideally, be a stimulator who gets his students to talk. Of course, when training a class to listen and understand, you have to speak more, but try and strike a balance. It's worth getting someone to come into your class with a stop watch, so that you can find out exactly how much talking you do.

Write clearly
Clear blackboard work is essential. If you can't write clearly on the blackboard, practise until you can. If you've got a lot to put on the board, try and arrange it in an orderly and logical fashion, so that the whole pattern is clear.

Encourage your students
There are few things so disarming as to find that you can talk no better in a foreign language than a child of two or three – especially if you're an adult student. As a teacher, therefore, encourage as much as possible. Say 'Good' or 'Good but ...' as often as you honestly can. Remember too that you can be encouraging or discouraging simply with intonation. The student will feel less discouraged if you, when rebuffing a wrong answer, say 'No' rather than 'No'.

Be careful with the use of grammatical terms
It's better to use as few of these as possible, apart from common ones like 'noun', 'adjective' and 'verb'. Many native speakers don't know what a conjunction is, nor the difference between a gerund and a participle. One difficulty about using names of tenses is that students will translate them. French people, for instance, will think the Present Perfect is the 'Parfait', although the two tenses function in very different ways. You should, however, be fully conversant with the terms yourself, particularly if you are teaching advanced students, or grammar-conscious nationalities.

Encourage your students to practise English outside the classroom

Often, a teacher makes less progress with his students, although he is competent in class, simply because he does not get his students to do homework and to read books, outside the classroom. The classroom should in fact act as a generator to all sorts of English studies outside it. Make your students feel appreciated when they hand in their homework. Don't forget B.B.C. broadcasts, English and American newspapers, English and American clubs. Try, too, to get your students to read English books for enjoyment rather than for new vocabulary.[1] English outside the classroom proves they can use the language in real life and therefore makes your lessons more appreciated. If you're teaching in England or America, get your students to buy a newspaper and read it on the way to school. At the beginning of each lesson, ask the class about the latest news. To begin with, only a small proportion may buy newspapers, but by the end of a week, many of them may have got into the habit, and this will add an extra twenty minutes to their English studies.

Take account of different levels within the class

Ideally, there should be enough chance of promotion or demotion from class to class for this not to be a problem. However, school organisation often cannot cope with this, and even a class where the level is fairly uniform will have differences with particular skills: one student will understand better and write worse than the others; another will have a larger vocabulary but bad pronunciation, and so on. There are a number of ways of dealing with the problem: ask difficult questions to the brighter students and then ask the same question later to those who lag behind. Get students to teach each other and talk about what they know to those who don't. Sit a more advanced student next to a less advanced one so that he can help. Do group work where you mix brighter students with those who know less. Try and get those who are behind to do more homework and more English outside the classroom. Encourage the less advanced student as much as possible and find out if there are areas where she/he is good so that you can call on him/her to show his/her knowledge. With a class of mixed nationality, get the Swede, say, to explain to the Spaniard a point which is easy for Swedes and difficult for Spaniards. At intermediate or advanced levels it is sometimes worth getting students up to teach a point which they have prepared. The class will probably be more interested in listening to one of themselves than to you, and one of the best ways of learning a language, paradoxically, is to teach it.

Deal with individual problems

It is often best to deal with individual problems after the class. The student concerned will feel that you really care about his progress if you spend additional time on him, and it is obviously much easier to get to the root of any problem in a *tête à tête* than in a large class.

1   See Appendix C.

Correct your students

Much depends here on the situation in class. However, even in the middle of a discussion in English it is possible to state the correct phrase or word, gently, while not interrupting the student. It is also helpful to note down mistakes and then to go over them at the end of the discussion. This is particularly useful with advanced classes, where students refuse to believe they need remedial work unless you *show* that they still make elementary mistakes.

Pair and group work

To give more practice in spoken English to your class, break them up into pairs or small groups. This encourages those who are shyer or reluctant to participate. With bigger classes, it can also stimulate conversation, although close supervision is necessary.

Use their names correctly

If you are teaching other nationalities, make sure you pronounce your students' names correctly. If you don't they may begin to feel that you are hardly in a position to correct their pronunciation. If you have a lot of different nationalities, get to know something about the countries they come from. If you think that the capital of Colombia is Lima, the Colombian student will feel that, as you are so ignorant about that, you are probably ignorant about other things as well. If he is sensitive, he may also feel that you are slighting his country.

Further reading

Littlewood, W., *Communicative Language Teaching*, CUP, 1983.

Discussion

1 Why is going methodically round the class with questions or exercises undesirable?

2 What techniques would you use to cater for different levels in a class?

3 Why is it important to encourage your students and how can you do this?

4 What are the disadvantages of using grammatical terms in class?

5 Do you think you should correct students all the time?

6 How can you make sure of including everyone in your class?

Exercises

1 Make a list of the ways in which you can stimulate the study of English outside the classroom.

2 Make plans to show ideal classroom seating for different activities.

3 Make a list of the points you have to consider when asking questions.

3 Teaching language skills

Just as students fail exams because they do not answer the questions precisely, so teachers of English fail when they do not know *why* they are teaching something. It is easy to become so used to time-tables that the reasons for using a dictation or comprehension passage are not considered – much less discovered. Learning a language usually has a practical aim – to enable students to communicate in that language. It is essential therefore that every minute of every class be directed to equipping students with the language skills they really need.

3.1. Principles

3.1.1. Functions

There are four primary language skills: Speaking, Understanding, Reading and Writing (see 1.3.). It is important to distinguish between them as they demand varied abilities, particularly as English pronunciation is so different from its written form. Thus, giving a talk requires different abilities to understanding a talk given by someone else, to presenting the same information in written form – or to reading what someone else has written on the subject.

Within the main skills there are a large number of functions. This is a term which describes the language you need to communicate and express yourself in different situations, which often overlap and reinforce one another.

If from the outset, the teacher decides the particular kinds of practice the students need, it can then be blended with the teaching of structure, idiom, vocabulary and pronunciation.

The following is a list of some functions which determine the way students need to form or react to language when speaking, understanding, reading or writing:

1 Giving and understanding instructions.
2 Giving and understanding messages.
3 Agreeing and disagreeing.
4 Persuading.
5 Refusing.
6 Asking the way.
7 Introducing.

8   Inviting.
9   Thanking.
10 Congratulating.
11 Expressing surprise.
12 Reassuring.
13 Encouraging.
14 Apologising.
15 Complaining.
16 Criticising.

If, from the outset, the teacher decides the particular kinds of practice his students need, he can then blend them with his teaching of structure, idiom, vocabulary, and pronunciation.

3.1.2. Register

All the above are affected by register, which is the way different language is used depending on whom you are talking to. For example, the way you persuade a child to do something requires a different linguistic approach to persuading your boss to do something. Selling from door to door is not the same as selling something to a business man at lunch. Each situation involves a different selection of structure, vocabulary, pronunciation, degree of formality and so on.

3.2. Application

Students need to be given practice in the use of different skills and different registers through situational dialogues and role-playing. Your selection of skills will be influenced by the language areas your students need to know. If you are teaching a group of doctors and practising ways of agreeing and disagreeing, you might have to create a situation where 'doctors' discuss the course of treatment a 'patient' should have. The register used from professional to professional – in this case 'doctor' to 'doctor' will be different from that of professional to client – 'doctor' to 'patient'. If you are teaching a class of business men, monologue practice could take the form of reports relating to each student's particular business interests, while if you are practising telephone conversations, sending or interpreting telegrams, writing or understanding letters, you would probably give them a business content. If you have a group of students from abroad who are going to study at English universities, you would probably give them practice in understanding lectures, in seminar discussions, and in writing compositions about their special subjects. You might also give them practice in understanding rapid speech, in criticism, in agreeing and disagreeing, in interjecting and in precise descriptions. You would, presumably, get them to discuss their special subjects and use the kind of register that would by used in academic discussions (see Further reading 2). As a second priority, you would probably choose the kind of secondary skills that might be needed for everyday life at a British university: asking the way, making telephone calls, being polite, thanking, inviting, persuading, refusing, and so on. So, where students have definite needs it is not difficult to determine the secondary skills you should teach, although these should be worked out methodically.

If, however, you are taking a general course in English, either for children or adults, you will probably have to plan and practise a larger number of secondary skills (to cover a wider and more general range of needs) and also determine when and how you are going to introduce them. As this is more difficult at beginners' level, where the language you use will have to be limited, here are a few examples:

'Persuading' and 'refusing' might have to be limited to simple intonation exercises with the words 'please' and 'I'm sorry':

Situation: A: Boyfriend.
             B: Girlfriend.

Dialogue: A: Come to the cinema tonight.
             B: Sorry!
             A: Please.
             B: I'm sorry.
             A: Why not. Come on.
             B: I can't!
             A: Please.
             B: No!

'Disagreeing' may have to be confined to simple practice of the present tense of 'to be':

Situation: A: Father.
             B: Son.

Dialogue: A: You're lazy.
             B: I'm not.
             A: You are!
             B: I'm not!
             A: You are!!
             B: I'm not!!

A telephone conversation would have to be extremely simple:

Situation: A: Mary's mother.
             B: Mary's boyfriend.
                Mary is not at home.

Dialogue: A: Hello.
             B: Hello. Is that Mrs Campbell?
             A: Yes. Who's that?
             B: John.
             A: Oh, yes.
             B: Is Mary there?
             A: No, sorry.
             B: Oh, thank you.

    A: Goodbye.
    B: Goodbye.

(For methods of presenting these dialogues see Chapter 8.)

From the beginning, then, this kind of practice not only trains students to speak in certain situations, but also means consolidating structure, vocabulary and idiom in an interesting way, while getting students to express realistic personal attitudes – an essential aim of language teaching.

Further reading

1 On the social functions of language and register: Wilkins, D. A., *Linguistics in Language Teaching*, Arnold, 1973.

2 On the particular needs of overseas students coming to British universities: *English for Academic Purposes*, ed. Cowie, A. P. and Heaton, J. B., a BAAL/SELMOUS publication, 1977.

3 Wilkins, D. A., *Notional Syllabuses*, O.U.P., 1976. Chapters 2 and 3.

4 Johnson, K. and Morrow, K., *Communication in the Classroom*, (Introduction only), Longman, 1981.

5 Revell, J., *Teaching Techniques for Communicative English*, Macmillan, 1979.

Discussion

1 What functions would the following students need to master and how could you give practice in them?

(a) a group of telephonists working at the switchboard of a large company that does a lot of business with other countries;

(b) a group of students studying English because they want to use it as tourists – on holiday abroad;

(c) a group of Science students (not in an English-speaking country) where lectures are in their native language, but much of the background literature is available only in English;

(d) a group of business men who are going to a conference on advertising in the United States.

2 In whàt situations could you practise 'encouraging' with an intermediate class?

Exercises

1 Write a short dialogue bringing out 'complaining' and 'apologising' at intermediate level, set in a hotel.

2   Make a list of the basic language items a foreigner might need if he found himself in the following situations:

   (a) booking a hotel room;

   (b) asking the way;

   (c) reporting an accident to the police.

4 Teaching structural patterns

4.1. Analysis

4.1.1. Principles

From a foreign learner's point of view, English grammar has certain advantages. The conjugation of verbs is relatively simple and there are no problems with gender. Initially, the major difficulty is the difference between pronunciation and written forms. Otherwise, English is a language that can be acquired more rapidly in the early stages than many others. At intermediate and advanced stages, however, everything becomes more confusing because rules are complicated by idiomatic exceptions.

In addition, the native English teacher often has the disadvantage of not having studied the grammar of his own language, as English school education does not always delve into it. The trainee teacher therefore has to learn to analyse structures which many of his students know better than he does.

Another consideration the teacher has to bear in mind is the language of his students. To take one example, 'I smoke' and 'I'm smoking' is a greater problem for a Swede than for a Spaniard, because no similar distinction exists in Swedish whereas it does in Spanish. The teacher, then, also has to learn the contrasts and similarities between English and his students' language(s).

He must also remember that it is difficult to teach any aspect of language in isolation and that the grammar he is presenting may also have problems involving pronunciation, spelling, different uses and forms, which will have to be taken into consideration and clarified.

Fortunately, the teacher has the textbooks he is using and various other reference books to help him (see end of chapter). However, the more he works things out for himself, the better will he remember how the language functions and the more will he acquire the habit of analysing it. He can then work out simple explanations for his students, avoiding where possible the use of grammatical terms, unless the students are already familiar with these.

4.1.2. Working out explanations

If there is a point you wish to explain to your pupils, try working it out for yourself by deductive analysis.

Example: the difference between 'remember to do something'
$$(remember + to + infinitive)$$
and 'remember doing something'
$$(remember + -ing form)$$

Think of some examples:

A: She remembered to $\left\{ \begin{array}{l} \text{turn off the electricity.} \\ \text{lock the house up.} \\ \text{feed the cat.} \end{array} \right\}$

23

B: She remembered {posting the letter.
                    putting the money in a drawer.
                    locking the house up.}

If you think about these examples and the situations, the explanation emerges:

A: 'remember to' – she didn't forget to turn off the electricity.
B: 'remember doing' – she remembered that she had done it.

In the first case she remembered to do something that was in the future:

She remembered that she had to do it.   She did it.

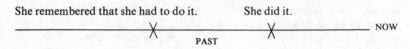

In the second, she remembered doing something in the past:

She did it.   She remembered doing it.

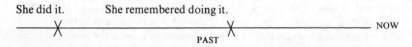

To take another example, if one wanted to explain the difference between 'after' and 'afterwards', one could simply say that 'after' is a preposition and 'afterwards' an adverb. However, this statement would probably not be of help to most students. Some purely practical explanation would probably be better:

Formula: 'after' refers to something coming later in the sentence.
             'afterwards' refers to something coming earlier in the sentence.

Contrasts: I had a cigarette after lunch.
               I had lunch. Afterwards I had a cigarette.

Try, too, to involve your students in this process of deduction. If you do so they will understand the point more clearly. Give them contrasting sentences for instance and ask them to explain the differences. In revision get them to prepare short lessons on grammatical points and then teach the class. The more you involve your students, the more motivated they will be.

Sometimes it is not possible to analyse items into formulae like this – for example, you can not formulate rules for irregular verbs, they have to be introduced and practised in context. The same applies to verbs that are followed by the gerund (-ing) 'I enjoyed *seeing* that film', the infinitive 'He persuaded me *to do* it' and 'that ... should', 'They suggested *that we should go* for a walk'. It would be impossible to give rules for what verbs are followed by what constructions – you simply have to make your students aware of these and teach them through practice.

One source of confusion is a structure whose form remains the same, but which is used in different ways. In this case, the various usages must be carefully differentiated. An example, which is difficult for all nationalities, is:

The Present Perfect (I have been)

Let us look at the two different usages, 1 and 2.

1 This consists of variations on the essential idea that the Present Perfect describes something that started in the past and continues into the present. Thus, in English, we would say 'I've lived in London since Christmas', implying that I am still in London now. This basic idea can be applied in the following ways:

(a) *Formula:* We use the Present Perfect when the past has an immediate effect on the Present.
    Example: 'He's stolen my money and I'm furious.'

(b) *Formula:* We also use this tense when something has just happened.
    Example: 'She's just given me the letter.'

(c) *Formula:* We use this tense with 'never' and 'ever' if they link present and past with the idea of 'up to now'.
    Example: 'I've never been so happy!'
    'Have you ever been to Greece?'

(d) *Formula:* The tense is used in a similar way with the Future and pre-Future.
    Example: 'He'll come when he's finished his work.'

However, the Present Perfect can also be used in quite a different way.

2 *Formula:* We use the Present Perfect for an event which is totally in the past but only when we do *not* define when it happened.
   Examples: I've studied in Paris!'
   'I studied in Paris *last year*.'

If 1 and 2 are taught together or mixed up, students will be confused. When teaching one of them you, therefore, have to be careful not to give examples, or say sentences, which belong to the other category. To take another example:

Prepositions

Prepositions are difficult to use in any language. However, the situation is made more difficult by 'mother tongue interference'. Thus, '*in*' can best be translated by 'en' in Spanish. Yet 'en' can also be used where we would use 'on' or 'at'. Again, 'a' in Spanish or Italian means 'to', among other things. But because 'a' seems similar to 'at', a common mistake with these nationalities is to use 'at' instead of 'to': 'He goes *at* York every day.'

Somehow, therefore, we must find some kind of system and ensure that the students recognise English prepositions as words in their own right, which have different meanings in different circumstances. Fortunately, we find that as long as we distinguish between these different circumstances, English prepositions are used in a literal sense, at least in the elementary stage.

Place (Static)

Here, 'on' and 'in' are used in only one sense:

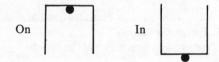

'At' is more complex but we can still find a consistent rule:

Ӿ   'At' is used when something is neither 'in' nor 'on', and when there is a sense of purpose connected with place:

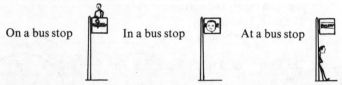

The little man is at a bus stop because he intends to take a bus. Otherwise he would be 'near' it. Similarly, people are 'at a school/church/university' or 'at home' because they are concerned with the function of those buildings, or areas. If we wanted to stress that someone is actually inside the building or on the roof, we would use 'in' or 'on'. If we emphasise study, worship, etc., we use 'at'. This brings out an essential point in the whole attitude to grammar: it is there to be used as the speaker wants.

We can also bring in 'look/smile/laugh at', here as indicating, a sense of direction, without movement, towards the person or thing, you laugh/smile/look at.

Having taught and consolidated this first stage as a definite rule, we can then get on to another concept.

Place (Movement)

Here 'at' can no longer be used as it does not describe movement. We can replace it by 'to'.

This again is a definite rule, although 'Put it on the table' is probably more common than 'put it onto the table'. Both, however are correct.

'Arrive at/in' might be thought to be an exception but, in fact, when we arrive, we are static, and 'arrive' is not therefore a verb of movement.

Finally, once this is understood and observed, we go on to the third stage:

Time

We are now going to use 'on', 'in' and 'at' in another sense where the words are the same but where the use is different – just as 'bark' can mean the skin of a tree, or the sound a dog makes. We can, however, find a slight link with previous uses of 'in', 'on' and 'at'.

At is used for the smallest units: At this moment/nine o'clock. ● At

On is used for the bigger units: On Tuesday/the 24th of May. On

In is used for the biggest units: In May/Spring 1975/the tenth century. In

Here, we do have to deal with exceptions which we can introduce as idioms, once the above is consolidated: 'at night', 'in a moment', 'at the weekend', 'in the afternoon'.

Fortunately, other prepositions such as 'near', 'between', 'under', 'over', 'above' are also literal and generally used for only one concept with place. Once we have taught this, however, we have to admit that the teaching of prepositions is idiomatic and piecemeal. How else are we to explain: 'to depend on', 'to be interested in', 'to be good at'?

Nevertheless, we have created as much order as possible. Furthermore, we have done it at the elementary stage so that our students are not plunged into anarchy right at the beginning. They will also realise, early on, that it is impossible to find the key through translation.

4.1.3. Selection of items to teach

The teacher must be able to select *which* structures to teach in what order (the most useful/easiest/those that lead naturally on to other structures, etc.).

As illustrated above with prepositions, a teacher must be able to think out the different aspects of a grammatical problem, and realise that in its entirety, it is too indigestible to be presented to the students, all at once. It is necessary to work out how to present it stage by stage at appropriate levels, and gradually build up the complete picture. As a complex instance of this, let us take the mass of different rules for the uses of 'some' and 'any'. The total definition can be summarised as follows.

– 'Some' can be used in positive sentences, although 'any' can also be used when it has the sense of 'any at all', i.e. 'any of these will do'. 'Any' rather than 'some' is used in negative sentences. 'Some' is used in questions when the answer 'yes' is expected and 'any' when the answer 'no' is expected. –

The presentation of this as one rule would lead to total confusion. Thus, it has to be broken up and introduced stage by stage at different levels, e.g.:

1   Beginners – 'some' in positive sentences in contrast to 'a', e.g. 'There are some biscuits in that box.'

2   Elementary – 'any' in negative sentences, e.g. 'There aren't any biscuits.'

3   Elementary – 'any' in questions, e.g. 'Have you got any biscuits?'

4   Elementary – 'some' with questions when you expect a positive answer, e.g. 'Can I have some biscuits please?'

5   Intermediate – 'any' in positive sentences, e.g. 'You can have any biscuits you like'.

Each time a new aspect of 'some' and 'any' is introduced, the previous forms can be practised again and consolidated. Each formula can be introduced as a definite rule which students must follow, and only later do you bring up alternatives or contradictions. This unfolding varies, depending on the text book you are using, or the students you are teaching. For instance, if you are teaching in an English speaking country, you might find it useful to introduce 'Can I have some . . . ?' at a much earlier stage, as it is a phrase students will need outside the classroom.

4.1.4. The effect of the learner's native tongue

An Englishman has no real reason to ask himself when we use 'the' and when we don't. He uses it when required, without thinking. However, all foreign learners find this question perplexing in varying degrees, depending on how far the usage in their language is different to English.

On the other hand, there is a lot of English usage which, because it is similar to other languages, does not really need to be explained at length. An example here is the simple use of the Pluperfect: 'He said he had made an appointment at eleven.' This, at least for most Europeans, should present few problems as usage is the same as in English.

Returning to 'the', let us examine when we use it in English and when we don't, and then try to discover why it is difficult for foreign learners.

'The'

The presumption is that students are already familiar with 'a/an' and the use of 'some/any'. Our analysis, therefore, is for intermediate levels. Hitherto, we have got our students to use 'the' in context without explanations. Now, however, we have to guide our students into using 'the' correctly, as their use of English is becoming more difficult. We use 'the' when we want to define:

A man
The man with a hat
The man with a tie
The man with one eye

Often the reason for definition need not be stated but can simply exist in the mind of the speaker:

'He's the man!'
'That's the necklace!'

This is fairly straightforward. However, the real difficulty is that most other languages use 'the' in particular circumstances in different ways from English, and that there is a whole range of languages such as Finnish, Arabic, Persian, Serbo-Croat and Japanese which do not use the definite article at all.

Thus, when analysing 'the' we have to discover which applications are difficult because of mother tongue interference.

Let us examine this in more detail. We start again with the general rule: *'We use "the" to define.'* Therefore, we never use 'the' when we are speaking in a general sense with any category, including the following:

WITH PLURALS
'Horses are not used much nowadays.'
However here, the French do use the definite article:
'On utilise peu *les* chevaux de nos jours.'

WITH UNCOUNTABLE NOUNS
'Steel is stronger than iron.'
Here the Italians would use a definite article:
L'acciaio e piu forte *del* ferro.'

WITH ABSTRACT NOUNS
'Life is a dream.'
The Swedes, do use the definite article, here:
'Liv*et* är en dröm.'

WITH MEALS
'We had a drink before dinner.'
The Germans differ here:
'Wir haben vor *dem* Abendessen etwas getrunken.'

WITH LANGUAGES
'English is spoken all over the world.'
The Portuguese would use the definite article, here:
'*O* ingles e falado em toda a parte.'

WITH SEASONS
'Autumn is my favourite season.'
Here the Spanish would use the definite article:
'*El* otoño es mi estación preferida.'

WITH DAYS OF THE WEEK
'I never go to the office on Saturday.'
The Rumanians use the definite article here:
'Eu nu merg nicadată la birou simbat*a*.'

English does not use the definite article with the following words used in a general sense. However, other languages *would* use the equivalent of 'the'.

'He stays *in bed* till ten.' 'Er bleibt bis um zehn Uhr *im Bett*.' (German)
'He goes *to church* regularly.' 'El merge *la biserică* regulat.' (Rumanian)
'Shall we stay *at home*?' 'On reste *à la maison*?' (French)
'I learnt that *at school*.' 'Ko ematha *sto skolio*.' (Greek)

Although these examples come under the main rule in English we must be aware of them, then, if they differ from the language of the students we are teaching. The following chart compares English with various languages in the above examples, as far as use of 'the' is concerned:

	Same usage as in English ✓ Different usage from English ×						
	Italian	German	Portug.	Swedish	Greek	French	Spanish
Plurals	×	×	✓	✓	×	×	×
Uncountables	×	×	✓	✓	×	×	×
Abstractions	×	×	✓	×	✓	×	×
Meals	✓	×	×	✓	✓	×	×
Languages	×	✓	✓	✓	×	×	×
Seasons	×	×	×	×	×	×	×
Days of the week	✓	✓	×	✓	×	×	×
'Bed'	✓	×	×	✓	×	×	×
'Church'	✓	×	✓	×	×	×	×
'Home'	✓	✓	✓	✓	×	×	✓
'School'	✓	×	✓	×	×	×	×

With the Japanese, Arabs, Turks, Serbo-Croats and Finns, the teacher has another task; not to teach them when to leave 'the' out, but when to put it in.

Unfortunately, the use of 'the' is only one example of the way usage in English contrasts with that in other languages. A teacher must therefore become aware of those areas where usage is different, and whether mother tongue interference is likely to occur.

SUMMARY

Above, you have various approaches which are used when analysing English grammar. There are, of course, many other structures to analyse in the course of your lessons. Train yourself to deduce the rule: adapt your analysis to the linguistic group you are teaching; find out what can be generalised and afterwards teach the exceptions and idiomatic uses; break your grammar into teachable formulae; build up from a structure your students know, to a new contrasting use; remember that if you present too many things too close together, your students will mix everything up. Remember, too, that you may begin with analysis but you should finish with so much practice and consolidation that the student no longer needs the rule, because he knows how to use structure without thinking about it – as do English people.

Fortunately, you have books to help you, and you will learn steadily by preparing your lessons, discussing points with other teachers and developing your own skill in breaking up the language, so that you can teach it effectively.

4.2. Application

4.2.1. Presenting structure

In the preceeding section we looked at some points a teacher needs to consider before presenting structures to his class.

The selection of structures to be presented is often decided for you by the structural grading of the book you are using, although you may introduce additional items at an earlier stage if you feel they are important for your students. It may also be easiest to build from other structures that your students already know. As an example, it is probably better to teach the Present Perfect in its continuous form, first, as your students have probably learnt 'I've' with 'I've got', and 'ing' with the Present Continuous. It is therefore easy to introduce 'I've' + 'been' + 'ing'. 'I've been living/studying/working etc. in London for two months'. Thus you teach a new tense with no new vocabulary except 'been', and without confronting them with the complex past participles of irregular verbs.

Structure teaching at advanced and intermediate levels often derives from items which have come up in reading or conversation, or involves explaining mistakes in composition and homework. In fact, this is probably the best approach as advanced level students often feel they know more than they do and are impatient with a formal presentation. An immediate ability on the part of the teacher to find ready answers is required here. However, if you feel you cannot give a clear explanation at once, tell your students you will deal with it later, and work out the answer in clear, incisive terms before the next class.

There are many ways of presenting structure and these are usually complementary rather than mutually exclusive. Vary your techniques as much as possible. Adapt your presentation to your class, and make sure it really is relevant to the point you are teaching. Make it vivid and precise and choose a form of presentation that leads naturally into practice.

In general, your presentation should be economical. Much more time should be spent on practice than on presentation. Meaning and form should be made obvious quickly. Otherwise your students will not understand what you want them to practise.

4.2.2.   Model sentences

These are sentences for oral practice which show the distinction between a point that your students already know and the new one that you are teaching them. If these sentences only contain vocabulary that your students already know, you can write them straight up on the board. For example, 'some' is already known to your students and you are introducing 'any' in negative sentences.

Model sentences: 'The butcher's got some lamb.'
'He hasn't got any bacon.'
'The newsagent's got some newspapers.'
'He hasn't got any stamps.'

From these examples the rule should be clear. In many ways however it is better to use model sentences in dialogue form, which make the sentences a natural exchange:

'I'd like some bacon please.' 'I'm sorry. We haven't got any bacon.'
'I'd like some lamb, please.' 'I'm sorry. We haven't got any lamb.'

You could follow on with various things that other shopkeepers have and haven't got, perhaps aided by visual material, and this would lead naturally into drills and dialogues.

When choosing your model sentences, try to make them relevant to your students' interests. For example if you are teaching a group of Iranian naval officers in preparation for a naval course they are going to do, you would bring in vocabulary that could be relevant:

'What furniture is there in the ward-room?'
'There are some tables, some chairs, some pictures on the walls.'
'There aren't any cupboards, any bunks, any desks etc.'

Model sentences can be presented on their own, or in combination with other things.

4.2.3.   Dialogues

You can introduce structures with straightforward dialogues where the meaning of a new structure is clear and where it is used appropriately. For instance, suppose you are introducing 'don't' with main verbs:

A: Excuse me, where's Piccadilly Circus?

B: Where? I don't understand.
A: Piccadilly Circus!
B: Oh – Piccadilly Circus. I don't know.
A: You don't know!
B: No. I don't live in London. I'm from Scotland.

The dialogue can be introduced on tape, then you can do repetition practice and get the class to act it out.

4.2.4. Situations

Presentation is always clearer and more meaningful if it is part of an actual situation or brief story. An obvious example when introducing 'going to' is preparing for a trip abroad: the teacher is going to visit England or America. What is he *going to do* beforehand?

$$I'm\ going\ to\ \begin{cases} \text{pack books, clothes, a toothbrush, etc.} \\ \text{say goodbye to your family.} \\ \text{take a bus to the airport.} \\ \text{etc.} \end{cases}$$

This leads naturally into what the students would do as individuals, 'I'm going to take my swimming costume because I like swimming' and to the use of different persons: 'Pepe's going to take his tennis racquet because he plays tennis.' The situation can also be set by using pictures. You can also introduce structures through situations created by sounds on a tape. These are fairly easy to record yourself. Use the real thing, or imitation. If for instance you want to introduce 'What is it/was it?' 'It was/is . . .', you can record or improvise the bark of a dog, the mew of a cat, the roar of a plane, and so on. This is also useful for the unfamiliar structure of 'It was' + noun + gerund. On the tape you can have the sound of someone typing, playing the piano etc.

'What was it?'
'It was someone typing/playing the piano', etc.
or
'What did you hear?'
'I heard someone typing.'
This idea can be developed to present other structures or new vocabulary.

4.2.5. Demonstration

Prepositions can be introduced effectively simply by placing things 'on' or 'in' or 'under' other objects. You put a key on the table, in your pocket, under a chair, etc., and describe where it is: 'It's under Pepe's chair', 'It's near his foot', 'It isn't on his chair', 'It's on the floor'.

An essential part of demonstration involves bringing things into the classroom. Thus when teaching 'I've got' you can bring in, and distribute, a whole range of objects which students have or haven't got.

Mime is also useful here, particularly as it makes students curious about what is going on. Thus, 'I'm 'eating', 'drinking', etc. can all be introduced effectively with mime; 'must' can be made clearer and more imperious with a pointing figure. 'Can' is effectively demonstrated in combination with 'lift': 'I can lift this chair/table/book etc.' 'I can't lift the radiator/carpet/door, etc.

4.2.6. Descriptions or narrative texts

You can produce a story or description with structure and vocabulary that the students already know, but introducing a new structure that is unfamiliar to them. This can be done very simply at an early stage. For instance, you want to introduce comparatives of adjectives to a group of Spaniards, so you produce a passage with general comparisons between Spain and Britain:

'The sun shines *more* in Spain than it does in Britain. It rains *less* and it is *warmer*. In Britain, there are *more* towns, and London, Birmingham, and Glasgow are *bigger* than Madrid or Barcelona. Spain produces *more* wine, rice, tomatoes than Britain, and Britain produces *more* cars.' etc.

Passages like this can easily be devised and they can also be made personal to the class. Be careful, though, not to introduce too much, or the passage becomes indigestible.

4.2.7. Grammatical statements

Let us take the difference between 'some' and 'any' again. If you are teaching students who speak European languages, you can use the terms 'negative' and 'positive', as the terms are familiar in their language. So you might write on the board:

'Some : positive sentences'
'Any   : negative sentences'

Here, you are using a simple shorthand for your rule. Supposing you write up: 'In positive sentences we tend to use "some" while in negative sentences we use any.' You will then be producing something less striking and more diaphanous, and your students at this stage will probably not understand 'tend' or 'while'. If you are presenting your rule to Arab students, they will probably not understand 'positive' and 'negative'. You could here perhaps use something more simple:

'Some : *Yes* sentences'
'Any   : *No* sentences.'

4.2.8. Diagrams

These can be useful in certain cases. With the Present Perfect, for instance, if you want to emphasise that it is used in both present and past:

'I've lived in London since Christmas.'
Christmas ← — — — — — — —Now.

To show the difference between 'since' and 'for':

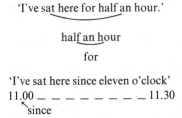

'I've sat here for half an hour.'

half an hour

for

'I've sat here since eleven o'clock'
11.00 _ _ _ _ _ _ _ _ 11.30
since

Diagrams are particularly useful for prepositions:

On   In   Off   Under   Above   Over

4.2.9. Drawing

The essential difference between usage can often be conveyed with simple drawings. To reinforce the idea of 'say' as words coming out of a mouth and 'tell' as communication between people, you could draw:

You could also synthesise the difference between 'make' and 'do' as follows: 'Do' is used with something that is already there, in the mind or in fact. On the other hand, we make something that was not there before. e.g. Make a cake/a fortune/a fuss/a noise, etc. Do homework/an exercise/a favour, etc.

You don't have to be an expert at drawing. Simple pin men can be effective.

4.3. Oral drills

After presentation and explanation of the new structure, students may need controlled practice in saying useful and correct sentence patterns in combination with appropriate vocabulary. These patterns are known as oral drills. They can be inflexible: students often seem to master a structure in drilling, but are then incapable of using it in other contexts. Drills, therefore, should open the way to other forms of practice which are dealt with later in this book. To summarise, drills should be:

1   Realistic – don't get students to practise sentences they would never actually say in real life.

2   Meaningful – practice should take place within a context – if possible relating to the students' interests.

3   Said with appropriate expression, e.g. surprise, impatience, enthusiasm, indifference, etc.

4   Used for only a minute or two. Use signs and pictures and sound prompts to give briskness and interest to the practice.

5   Used as a first stage, quickly leading the way to other kinds of practice.

4.3.1.   Types of drills

4.3.1.1.   LISTENING AND REPETITION DRILL

Technique: The teacher says the sentence he wants the students to practise several times with the same intonation and stress. The students imitate him exactly. Anything can be practised with this drill, and, because it's simple, it's useful as a first stage.

Objective: to practise 'needn't have'.

Teacher: 'It didn't rain, so I needn't have taken my umbrella.'

   (Perhaps holding an umbrella, to give context.)

Repeat several times.

Students: 'It didn't rain so I needn't have taken my umbrella.'

   (Pass the umbrella to each student as he speaks.)

4.3.1.2.   SIMPLE SUBSTITUTION DRILL

Technique: Give the basic sentence pattern. The students are then required to substitute different items in a given place in the sentence. As it requires the substitution of only one item this drill is also rather simple.

Objective: to practise 'Did you see . . .?'

Key/Model sentence: Did you see that aeroplane?

   Teacher says several times, Students repeat.

Prompt: (Teacher gives word or shows/   *Students:*
draws/or points to a picture)

aeroplane	Did you see that aeroplane?
car	Did you see that car?
bus	Did you see that bus?
etc.	

4.3.1.3.   VARIABLE SUBSTITUTION DRILL

Technique: Give the model sentence, then the prompt they are to substitute, which requires them to think about and change something in the rest of the sentence.

Objective: you want them to practise the use of 'was/were'.

Prompt:	*Students:*
I was at school	I was at school
John	John was at school
John and Mary	John and Mary were at school

The stress will be on the new prompt. Here, make sure of the weak form with 'was'. You could perhaps elicit an indignant response, by prompting with an accusation.

Prompt:	*Students:*
John wasn't at school	John *was* at school.
John and Mary weren't at school.	John and Mary *were* at school.
and so on.	

4.3.1.4. PROGRESSIVE SUBSTITUTION DRILL

Technique: Give the model sentence. Then give prompts that have to be substituted in different parts of the sentence and which may require alteration of other words. As this drill is more complicated, it is not so useful for initial practice but is ideal for the quick revision of different points, and really makes students think.

Objective: to practise the first conditional, at the same time revising 'will/won't' and the third person of the simple present.

Key/Model sentence: If John argues I'll be angry.

Prompt:	*Students:*
Mary	If Mary argues, I'll be angry.
smoke	If Mary smokes, I'll be angry.
they	If Mary smokes, they'll be angry.
furious	If Mary smokes, they'll be furious.
Jane	If Jane smokes, they'll be furious.
disagree	If Jane disagrees, they'll be furious.

The student has to work out where the prompt goes in the sentence. If there are two alternative places, he can choose between them. For instance, with the prompt 'they' in the above, the response could be 'If Mary argues, they'll be angry' or 'If they argue, I'll be angry'. Don't go so .fast that the students are confused, but do get them accustomed to rapid decisions and reactions. Notice that the stress usually comes on the prompt.

4.3.1.5. SITUATIONALISED DRILL

Technique: Give an example using the set phrase or structural item you wish to practise. Give prompts that elicit this response. Go on to paired practice.

Objective 1: to practise the phrase 'That is bad luck'.

Prompt:	*Students:*
I've broken my leg.	That is bad luck.
I've failed my exams.	That is bad luck.

The first speaker might express courageous resignation while the second expresses genuine concern.

Objective 2: to practise 'I've never . . .'.

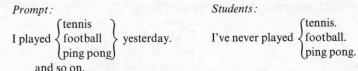

Prompt: *Students:*

I played $\left\{\begin{array}{l}\text{tennis} \\ \text{football} \\ \text{ping pong}\end{array}\right\}$ yesterday.   I've never played $\left\{\begin{array}{l}\text{tennis.} \\ \text{football.} \\ \text{ping pong.}\end{array}\right.$

and so on.

You could, perhaps, establish the theme of sport with a cut-out or illustration on the board. Perhaps make the first speaker pleased with himself and the second one off-hand.

4.3.1.6.   QUESTION AND ANSWER

Technique: In class there is a tendency to practise responses more than questions. So start off yourself and then get students to form the questions themselves. Make sure they get the right intonation and that the answers are naturally phrased. This can be used to practise almost anything, but, therefore, don't use too much.

Objective: to practise 'How many_____are there?'

Prompt: *Students:*

                 One.

How many $\left\{\begin{array}{l}\text{windows} \\ \text{doors} \\ \text{pictures}\end{array}\right\}$ are there in the classroom?   Two.

                 Three.

Remember the answers should be natural – here 'two' or 'one' is much more usual than 'there are two', etc.

4.3.1.7.   CLAUSE COMBINATION

Technique: Give an example, e.g. two sentences; then show how these can be combined into one. This can be used for complex sentences and is therefore good with advanced classes. Useful for making students aware of how they can say the same thing in different ways.

Objective: 'The _____ whose.'

Prompt: He's a postman. His wife died the other day.

Response: He's the postman whose wife died the other day.

Prompt: He's a policeman. His son is at university.

Response: He's the policeman whose son is at university.

4.3.1.8.   TRANSFORMATION DRILL

Technique: Give a sentence that the students have to transform in some way, e.g. from a positive statement to a negative statement. This is particularly useful for comparing positive, negative, and interrogative forms.

Prompt: *Response:*

I've got a red car.   Have you got a red car?

She's got a new bicycle.   Has she got a new bicycle?

  and so on.

This type of drill can be difficult to put into context, but in the above, for example, you could do it simply by stressing the adjective and introducing scepticism into the question form:

I've got a red car.   Have you got a RED car? and so on.

4.3.1.9. SUBSTITUTION DIALOGUES

Technique: Present dialogue (perhaps on tape). Practise and act out. Give prompts to be substituted in appropriate parts of the dialogue. Useful for vocabulary, idiom, and structure practice.

Objective: to practise frequency adverbs and revise pronouns as complements.

Model dialogue: A: You're always rude to Annie.
  B: I'm not. I'm sometimes rude to her.
  A: Well – you're never polite to her.
  B: I am. I'm often polite to her.

Prompts for substitution: John/Peter/Mary/your teacher
  unpleasant/pleasant
  nasty/nice
  unkind/kind and so on.

The attitudes here are self-evident. This leads easily into improvisation.

4.3.1.10. SUBSTITUTION TABLES

These are written on the board. The student chooses what he wants to say. You should be able to go through fairly fast, as long as the pronunciation is all right. Here is one which practises 'want + infinitive'. This structure is difficult because, like verbs of ordering and requesting, it is followed by the subjunctive in many languages. Here you have a total of 160 possible sentences:

My	guests			go to the cinema.
His	friends	want	to	swim.
Her	parents	wanted		listen to the radio.
Our	cousins			read.

Be careful when constructing tables, as it is very easy to produce strange combinations. Vocabulary should already be familiar, and attention has to be paid to stress. Decide on a mood, attitude or a situation. In the above example, it would be much better to produce a prompt, e.g. 'Let's go dancing!' You could then get the students to precede all the sentences with 'But', and make the tone one of protest.

Tables are also useful for simultaneous revision, or for practising idiomatic phrases – in this case: 'my', 'his', 'her', 'our', and the phrases 'go to the cinema' and 'listen to the radio'.

Substitution tables bridge speaking and reading. Once your students are familiar with a structure or with vocabulary, orally, they can consolidate spelling and pronunciation through reading appropriate sentences aloud.

Use tables for homework. If students have consistent problems with a structure, get them to write out a relevant table and repeat as many sentences as possible at home. Go over it beforehand in class, though, making sure that they can pronounce the sentences correctly.

In order to situationalise to a greater extent, you can have both a question and answer, but keep them short and simple. Here, we are practising the use of 'don't/doesn't' in negative sentences:

What's { wrong? the matter?	He She	doesn't	like	coffee. meat. tea. alcohol.
	I We They	don't		

One student asks the question, and another answers. With more advanced classes, these tables lead on naturally to improvisation, and your students can produce any sentence they want, as long as it incorporates the structure you are practising. Balloon tables can be used for testing:

This is particularly good for word order as the students have to 'assemble' each sentence.

James Duke suggests Prompting Tables from which students have to create sentences.[1] Here is one which practises 'was/were' and prepositions of Time and Place:

	At Christmas	On New Year's Day	In the Spring	Last weekend
Mr N.	Paris	Cairo	Rabat	at home
Mrs N.	London	Madrid	Osaka	in the garden
O. & P.	Rome	Bonn	Tahiti	on the beach

1   *Modern English Teacher*, Vol. 2, No. 3, 1974.

Sentences can be developed along a number of different patterns, e.g. 'While Mr M. was in Paris at Christmas, O. & P. were in Rome.' 'Where was Mrs N. last weekend? Was she in Madrid?', etc. You could also practise the future, or 'may/might'.

Ideally, of course, substitution tables should be completed by the students themselves, and should reflect their activities:

Mario Paul Pedro Gerlinda Yukiko Françoise	did didn't	do	his her	homework composition	last	Monday. night. week.

4.3.2. Signs

You can simplify the practice of drills by prompting with signs whose meaning you establish early on.

This is particularly useful for variable substitution with pronouns and tenses. Devise any system you like. Here is one:

Wave towards the student who is going to speak, with your left hand. Then, make the following signs for the pronoun you want him to use:

'I'   Thump your chest with your right hand.
'You'   Point forward with your right arm.
'She'   Point to the left with your left arm.
'He'   Point to the right with your right arm.
'We'   Extend your arms and wave your hands inwards.
'They'   Point both your arms forward.

To indicate different tenses:
'Present'   Point down towards your feet.
'Past'   Make a hitch-hiking sign over your right shoulder.
'Future'   Thrust your left arm forward.

The advantages of these signs is that your students pay greater attention in a drill, so as not to miss a sign. You can get a faster tempo, and avoid the continual intrusion of the teacher's voice. Devise your own for silent correction and frequent prompts.

4.3.3. Other prompts

Apart from speech and signs, there are other ways of providing prompts for drills. One of the most effective is by way of pictures or flash cards (see 10.4.). Another is from words written on the board. Many prompts for language laboratory exercises come from the tape, and it is also possible to indicate the tense you want by written signs on the board.

Prompts of this kind are also valuable because they bring variety, and you accustom the student to react in English to different things around him, whether written, spoken or seen.

Further reading

1   Reference books on English Grammar:
Close, R. A., *A University Grammar of English Workbook*, Longman, 1974.
Close, R. A., *A Reference Grammar for Students of English*, Longman, 1975.
Alexander, L. G., Stannard Allen, W., Close, R. A., O'Neill, R. J., *English Grammatical Structure*, Longman, 1975.
Thomson, A. J. and Martinet, A. V., *A Practical English Grammar*, O.U.P., 1960.
Palmer, F. R., *The English Verb*, Longman, 1974.
Leech, G., *Meaning and the English Verb*, Longman, 1971.
Swan, M., *Practical English Usage*, OUP, 1984.
Allsop, J., *English Grammar*, Cassell, 1984.

2   On methodology:
Finochiaro, M. and Bonomo, M., *The Foreign Language Learner*, Regents Publishing Co., 1973.
Mackey, W. F., *Language Teaching Analysis*, Longman, 1965.

3   On drills:
Dakin, J., *The Language Laboratory and Language Learning*, Longman, 1973.
Finochiaro, M. and Bonomo, M., *The Foreign Language Learner*, Regents Publishing Co., 1973.
Mackey, W. F., *Language Teaching Analysis*, Longman, 1965.
Byrne, D., *Teaching Oral English*, Longman, 1986.

Discussion

1   What have you got to keep in mind if you are going to use oral drills effectively?

2   What are the respective advantages and disadvantages of using individual, pair or chorus work with drills?

Exercises

1   Write a short dialogue for a late elementary class to introduce the use of 'didn't' with main verbs.
2   Work out ways of presenting the following:

    (a) 'under' and 'above' used as static prepositions of place
    (b) 'some' and 'any' in questions
    (c) 'has/have got'.

3   Think of a short description or story you would use if you were presenting 'I've just' to a class of children aged 12–14. Use all the personal pronouns.

4   Give an example of a Progressive Substitution drill to practise the use of 'don't/doesn't' in negative sentences.

5   Construct a substitution table to practise 'when + present simple + future', e.g. 'When he goes, I'll tell you'. Work out the sequence for using it.

5 Teaching vocabulary

5.1. Choosing vocabulary

The vocabulary you introduce is to some extent conditioned by the books you are using, but you may choose to bring in other areas of vocabulary that you feel are relevant for your pupils. A distinction needs to be made between (a) *active* vocabulary – words which the student understands, can pronounce correctly and uses constructively in speaking and writing; and (b) *passive* vocabulary – words that the student recognises and understands when they occur in a context, but which he cannot produce correctly himself.

There is also a need to *limit* the vocabulary that is introduced – if too much is introduced, students will be impeded by the need to absorb too many words. Sometimes, both students and teachers assume the contrary because extensive lists of words 'covered' in a textbook or notebook give a sense of visible accumulation and, therefore, of 'progress'. This, though, is rather like trying to imagine a tree with no trunk and branches – but only leaves. Massive vocabulary without the structure, idiom, and expressiveness to carry it does not bring mastery of a language – just as a mass of leaves is not a tree, but a compost heap.

There are certain guidelines on which the choice of vocabulary can be based:

5.1.1 Commonest words
It is important to choose words that are commonly used, or words that students need. Any unusual word you teach will take the place of a useful one in the student's mind. The teacher is helped here by the textbook where vocabulary is graded, and lists of the commonest words are also available.

5.1.2 Students' needs
If a student wants to know a special word, it is usually worth teaching it to him because motivation will ensure that he remembers it. However, don't teach it to the whole class unless they will all find it useful. If, for instance, a student is passionately interested in butterflies and wants to know all the English names for all the parts of a butterfly's body, it is probably best to suggest he does some research on his own with a dictionary, unless the rest of the class are also entymologists!

As has been stated earlier, knowing your students' background is of help. It will give you an idea of what words your students are most likely to need or want to know.

You may have a class in a company, or students who want to learn technical English. Remember that the essence of teaching here still depends on structure, idiom and expressiveness. Most businessmen and technical experts also need their English to get around other countries, to give and take hospitality, and to chat to colleagues at conferences. A lot of technical and commercial English is, in any case, also international.

However, your students will feel frustrated if you teach vocabulary which they feel they do not need. Even at beginner's level, it is better to choose particular words connected with their work or profession. You might, for instance, find it better to provide the vocabulary connected with an office rather than a home. Instead of the countryside, it might be more rewarding to choose words connected with the place they work in.

Thus, choosing specialised vocabulary is often a question of slanting your teaching in a particular direction, rather than teaching nothing but specialised words.

A real problem arises when you have a class with students who are each interested in a different aspect of commercial or technical English. At beginner's level you will probably be teaching them general English, perhaps choosing words that are common to their different professions. At intermediate or advanced levels, you will have to explain that you cannot go into everyone's specialised vocabulary in depth because it would not be useful to the others, but that you will try to choose general, commercial or technical terms which everyone finds useful. You can then draw out the individual's speciality by getting each of them to tell the class about their work.

Group work is also useful here: get the lawyers, the bankers, the insurance men into groups and get them to work out projects involving vocabulary which applies to their own speciality. It's essential here, that you yourself know as much about each profession as possible so that you have some common ground with each group.

5.1.3. Students' language

If you are teaching a class from one language group, a knowledge of their language will tell you which words are similar in their language and English, and therefore easily learnt. For example, when teaching Frenchmen, Spaniards or Italians, it is likely that English words that have a Latin origin will be similar to the French, Spanish, or Italian word. There are also a large range of commercial and technical words which co-exist in all languages.

On the other hand, you need to be careful with words that sound the same in the students' language, but in fact mean something quite different in English – for example, 'also' in German, means 'thus'; 'novela' is a 'short story' in Italian; 'actuellement' means 'now' in French; 'sensible' is 'sensitive' in Spanish; 'överta' in Swedish is not to 'overtake', but to 'take over'.

Remember, too, that similar words have different intensities in other languages. The equivalent of 'stupid' ('estupido') in Spanish is a much greater insult than the equivalent in English. Value words like 'family', 'friend', 'shame', can be translated literally but have different cultural nuances, and it is difficult to find an equivalent for the word 'cosy' outside Northern European languages, or for 'simpatico' in English.

Particular pronunciation difficulties may also affect your choice of vocabulary and make it more complicated than you thought: 'get' for Spaniards because the 'g' is difficult; 'horse' for Italians because the 'h' is too easily omitted; 'woman' for Germans because they want to pronounce the 'w' as 'v'; 'very' for the Japanese because they pronounce 'r' as 'l'; in French, word stress is often on the third syllable: secre**taire**: **se**cretary. It may be better therefore, to drill sounds, or practise stress patterns before presenting certain words.

5.1.4. Word building
It is often worth choosing a word because a general rule can be formed, e.g. teach-teacher, work-worker, etc. Another instance is the fact that most words ending in 'ion' have the same meaning in European languages: 'revolution', 'constitution', 'abstraction', etc.

5.1.5. Topic areas
In many ways, it is easier to teach vocabulary which belongs to one area of sequence, as the student will be able to form a pattern of interrelated words in his mind. Beware, however, of being carried away by the teaching situation. You are, for instance, going through a short dialogue with an elementary class in a doctor's consulting room. Your object is to teach phrases which could give them a useful basis: 'I'm not well', 'What's wrong?' 'I've got a pain here'. From these, you could also produce a limited number of alternatives: 'I'm ill', 'I've got a headache/a pain in my leg/arm, etc.'. You get your students to act out these variations, and perhaps end up with the 'doctor' pretending to write out a prescription and saying 'Take this to the chemist'. However, you may find yourself carried away by the fact that one new word leads naturally to another, and before you know where you are, you also produce as many diseases as Pandora did when she opened her box. Your students will probably welcome this because they feel they are learning a lot quantitatively, but in fact your students will forget, or never use, most of what you are teaching them.

5.1.6. Cross reference
A lot of words are applicable to different situations or specialisations. If, for instance, you are choosing vocabulary connected with cars, it is worth choosing terms that are also common to other means of transport, such as trains, aeroplanes, taxis, buses. You thus make the application wider and more useful and you can revise the vocabulary later in different situations.

Cars, Trains, Aeroplanes etc

brake	electricity	passenger	speed
crash	m.p.h.	petrol	start
door	oil	roof	stop
engine	park (vb)	seat	window

In contrast, there are words that are less useful because they cannot be used widely in other contexts:

Cars: tyres, gear, clutch, etc.
Aeroplanes: undercarriage, aileron, joy-stick, etc.
Trains: guard, van, compartment, etc.

There are, of course, a number of words with narrower application which might be introduced as long as there are not too many pronunciation difficulties, because they are internationally known: pilot, jet, airport, piston, diesel, etc.

Once you have provided your students with a general basis of vocabulary which touches on as many different spheres as possible, they should be able to fit in more specialised vocabulary later on when they need it.

5.1.7. Related structures

Many structures 'demand' their own vocabulary. Thus, if you're teaching 'have got' you will tend to choose the names of personal possessions. If you are teaching 'going to' you are likely to introduce a vocabulary connected with plans. If you are teaching the Present Continuous you will want to introduce active verbs with their corresponding objects. This is the most 'natural' way to choose vocabulary, but you have still got to be careful that you choose common words, and not too many of them.

5.2. Presenting new vocabulary

Before presenting vocabulary in class, it is helpful to remember the following:

1 Whenever possible, teach the words in spoken form first, and only when your students can pronounce them well, introduce the written form. Otherwise, your students will always try and pronounce English words as if they were written in their own language, and it will be difficult for you to break this.
2 Try to present new words in context.
3 Revision is essential. Blend words you have presented into later practice.

If you introduce new words which are not in the textbook you are using, jot them down in a notebook so that you can bring them up again. There are many ways of presenting new vocabulary. Here are some of them:

5.2.1. In context

If the word occurs in a text or passage, the meaning can often be deduced when the other words in the sentence are already known:

e.g. ... fall from the trees in autumn.
      A young cow is a ...

This deductive process applies particulary to the use of reading passages or stories, whether taped, read or told.

5.2.2. Create a context

The only way to teach the meaning of many abstract words is by creating a context or situation from which the students can then deduce the meaning. Take the meaning of the word 'brave'. If you are teaching French students you know that 'brave' in French means 'honest' or 'worthy', so you will have to be very exact. Create a character who is brave. Accompany your example by mime or drawing if necessary: 'There was a house on fire and he went in and saved a girl on the top floor.' Don't worry if your examples seem trite, as long as they are clear and vivid – it's better to be precise, here, than obscure and original. You can also use characters known to your student: someone read about in a newspaper or from history. With Italians: 'Garibaldi was brave because he landed in Sicily with only a thousand men.' With French students: 'Napoleon was brave because he led his men across the bridge at Arcoli.' etc. Be careful though that the meaning is exactly understood. Some situations could be misinterpreted – for example some students might think that Garibaldi was 'stupid' to land with only a thousand men!

5.2.3. Descriptions or definition

You can also describe and define objects, although drawing is often more effective: 'You steer a ship with a *rudder*', 'You put luggage into the *boot* of a car', 'A *lawn* is an area of grass in a garden'.

5.2.4. Outside the classroom

Take your class out and introduce words for things seen in a shop window, or in the street. Close control and plenty of revision is needed here but it is a vivid way of teaching, and new vocabulary is taught in a living context.

5.2.5. Objects

There are hundreds of simple objects already in the classroom, others which can probably be seen through the window, and others which can be brought in when needed. These can be simple or complicated, from forks and spoons to using things, like machinery, which can be taken to pieces and assembled again for specialised classes.

5.2.6. Drawing

Even a teacher without too much skill can represent simple objects on the board. If he draws badly, a guessing game ensues to determine what he actually has drawn.

5.2.7. Mime

This is particularly useful for actions: 'eating', 'drinking', 'jumping', 'tripping up', etc. It can also involve the objects connected with these verbs: 'drinking coffee', 'eating a sandwich', etc. Revise by getting your students to mime when you say a word.

5.2.8. Opposites

A word can often be defined if the students know its opposite: 'A brave man isn't afraid' 'An ugly girl isn't pretty' 'A plain girl isn't pretty or ugly' etc.

5.2.9. Synonyms

As words of Latin origin in English are often paralleled by those of Anglo-Saxon origin and vice versa, synonyms can be useful for students from 'Latin' countries, or for Germans or Scandinavians. A French student may understand 'brave' if you say it is the same as 'courageous'. A German student may understand 'commence' if in your definition you bring in the word 'begin'.

5.2.10. Translation

Taking the word 'brave' again, it could be argued that it would be much simpler to translate the word with a mono-lingual class, without bringing in Garibaldi, or a burning house. Certainly, there is much less objection to translating individual words than to doing this with structure and idiom, particularly if you are in a hurry. With a class of different nationalities, however, you may find it difficult to translate into all the necessary languages. Also, the quest for the meaning of a word through situations makes it more memorable when the student does eventually discover what it is. If you do translate vocabulary, make sure you then exemplify the word in context, or your students will forget it easily. As equivalent words are not always used in exactly the same way in different languages, setting them in context also brings out their exact meaning.

5.2.11. Pictures/flash cards

The existence of a wide assortment of magazines and illustrated advertisements means that pictures can be easily found for special vocabulary areas such as kitchens, clothes, cars, interiors and so on. The pictures or cuttings can be pasted on to a piece of cardboard to make a flash-card (see 10.4.).

5.2.12. Wall charts (see 10.5)

These are valuable because they also present vocabulary in a visual context, as long as they are clearly visible. One way of presenting vocabulary through them is as follows:

(a) Take an area of the wall chart and identify some objects – ten at most – without writing up anything. Get students to repeat and familiarise themselves with the pronunciation.

(b) Point at the objects, and get students to tell you what they are.

(c) Once students are familiar with the vocabulary and can pronounce it, write up the words on the board.

(d) Point at objects again and get students to read the corresponding word from the board.

(e) Rub out the words. Point at the objects and get students to spell them orally, or on the board.

(f) Get the students to use the vocabulary they have learnt, to describe part of the wall chart.

In this way, you get the students to repeat the vocabulary and yet sustain their interest by approaching it from different teaching angles. Finally, you get them to integrate the words through description. To revise, a few days later, just put the wall chart up again, and go through a similar process quickly. This approach can of course be varied with questions, descriptions of the objects themselves, with contradictions, etc.

5.2.13. Word games

There are a large variety of these and they are useful for practising and revising vocabulary after it has been introduced. Crossword puzzles are useful, particularly for group work, or as homework. So is Scrabble with a very small advanced class. 'Animal–Mineral–Vegetable' can also be lively, although it is best to define your type of question here: '*Is it* blue etc.?' '*Can you* find it in the country/town/sea etc.?' '*Do you* wear/smoke/drink it, etc.?' If you define the stages, you both suggest questions to students who cannot think of any, and ensure the practice of the structures you want.

There are also a number of word games that approximate more to exercises:

e.g.   Pair off related words:

corn	pencil
mouse	army
money	road
cup	cigarettes
street	cat
matches	bread
pen	saucer
General	bank

Or: Relate colours with nouns:

silver	a London taxi
blue	London buses
yellow	the sky in summer
red	grass
green	snow
white	the moon
black	butter

Most of these games, or puzzles, revise vocabulary that the students already know. However, they also point out areas of ignorance which students then want to fill. As a teacher, it is important to ask yourself *why* you are using these games and then fulfil your teaching objective, as efficiently as possible.

5.3.   Combining vocabulary teaching with structure and pronunciation revision

When new vocabulary is being introduced and practised, there is a good opportunity for the general revision of structure and pronunciation. If, for example, we are using a wall chart that represents the seaside, we can take the beach as our 'area'.

The new words are 'boat', 'sea', 'wave', 'child/children', 'bird', 'play(ing)', 'fly(ing)'. This is an elementary class and they have a limited amount of vocabulary and structure: colours; verbs like 'standing', 'sitting', 'eating', 'drinking'; interrogative pronouns: the Present Continuous: 'there is/are': 'this/that/these/those'; imperatives. After the teacher has introduced questions and statements, he gets the students, themselves, to speak as much as possible.

Don't go into the definite article and uncountable nouns. Get students up, pointing, identifying. Then start questions. Establish stress, intonation and sound-linking.

$$\text{That's} \begin{cases} \text{a BOAT/CHILD/BIRD/WAVE} \\ \text{the} \begin{cases} \text{SEA} \\ \text{SAND} \end{cases} \end{cases}$$

What's THAT? It's a BOAT etc.
Where's the BOAT? On the SAND etc.
What's the CHILD doing? PLAYing etc.

Colours	The SAND's YELLOW etc.
	What COLOUR is the sand? It's YELLOW.
	The SEA's YELLOW! It ISN'T. It's BLUE etc.
'There is/are'	There's a BOAT on the SAND etc.
	There's a BIRD in the SKY etc.
	What's in the SKY? etc.
Numbers	There are FOUR BOATS on the SAND.
	No, there AREN'T. There's ONE.
'How many?'	How many boats (etc.) are there?

Continue in this way with questions, statements and contradictions which link the new vocabulary to any structure or idiom you want to practise.

Once the vocabulary has been consolidated, you could leave it for some days and then go back to it with new structures. Your progress here is like a man walking: putting his weight on one leg to stride forward with the other. With new structures you revise 'old' vocabulary and with new vocabulary you revise 'old' structure.

5.4 Passive vocabulary

As this is vocabulary which the student understands but doesn't use, the teacher himself is not so concerned with it. However, a big range of passive vocabulary is invaluable to the student, particularly as time does not allow the introduction of a lot of words in class. The teacher's role, therefore, includes advising his students on the choice and use of a dictionary and getting them to read as much as possible. The dictionary should, preferably, be one which marks pronunciation, and it may be necessary to explain the phonetic system. There are a mass of Readers[1] produced by many publishers, and these should accompany any course.

Checking up on what has been done is the key to getting your students to acquire passive vocabulary — as with all other forms of homework. If you can keep a record of what should be revised, it will be of great help to you and the class.

When converting passive to active vocabulary, you will inevitably have to work on pronunciation, while setting up the words firmly in a context to ensure they are used properly.

5.5. Phrases, idioms and colloquial expressions

Many phrases, idioms and expressions which occur in everyday conversation are unknown to students who have been taught purely structurally – e.g. 'not at all', 'fine', 'not really', 'I don't mind', 'let me see', and so on. 'Softeners' are also valuable in that they help to produce natural conversation and make students aware of the difficult English habit of diluting definite statements: 'well', 'actually', 'of course', 'I'm afraid', 'don't you think?', 'I wonder if', 'on the whole', 'I *do* think', etc.

It is usually better to teach these as they emerge from conversation or in comprehension passages, and then revise them some time later in suitable situations.

Phrasal verbs are obviously an essential part of English, but it can be confusing to teach 'make up', 'make out', 'make into', 'make over' and so on all together in one lesson as students will confuse the particles. Much better to teach them one by one as they are needed, or if the student comes across them outside the classroom and asks for an explanation. Otherwise, half-digested as they may be, phrasal verbs become a brake to fluency and not an aid to it.

Presenting and consolidating an idiom depend essentially on finding a precise context, or being able to explain it with equivalents, or on being able to give a sufficient number of examples of its use. Then you have to check that your students can use it correctly.

Let us take the idiomatic phrase: 'on top of the world'. Let's say it appears in a dialogue where someone has just won a lot of money at the races. You introduce the alternatives:

$$\left.\begin{matrix} \text{'I'm feeling} \\ \text{'I feel} \end{matrix}\right\} \text{ on top of the world.'}$$

Context: Explain that he is on top of the world because his horse has won.
Equivalents: very happy, feels wonderful, ecstatic, etc.

1   See Appendix C.

Examples: Here you could prompt with simple situations to which the students respond:

He's passed his exam.	He's on top of the world.
She's got a good job.	She's on top of the world.
They've just had a son.	They're on top of the world.
We've just heard the good news.	We're on top of the world.

Checking: Get your students to produce examples, prompting if necessary. 'The holidays have begun', 'I've bought a new car', etc. Ask your students to invent sentences in pairs and then get them to tell the rest of the class. Or, get them to devise little dialogues with variations: 'You must be on top of the world', 'Don't you feel on top of the world?'

This example is fairly full. In fact, in class, you would probably not want to spend so much time on single idioms. You would perhaps give and elicit a few examples, check that students have understood, and then revise briefly with equivalents and other examples on successive days.

All this, of course, depends on how useful the particular item is. Avoid slang that is too colloquial or likely to go out of fashion, and discourage a tendency to labour colourful phrases. Remember the perpetual enemy: time. When embarking on something you have to ask yourself whether it is really useful to teach it, given that no one can spend their whole life learning English and that students can only absorb a limited amount each day.

Further reading

1 Wilkins, D. A., *Linguistics in Language Teaching*, Arnold, 1973. Chapter 4.

2 Gower and Walters, *Teaching Practice Handbook*, Heinemann, 1983.

3 Cairns, R., *Working with Words*, CUP, 1986.

Discussion

1 How would you go about choosing vocabulary for an advanced commercial class which consists of import/export managers, accountants and shipping agents?

2 What vocabulary would you choose at an early intermediate stage in order to help students go through Customs?

3 How would you deal with the student who wanted to know all the different parts of a car engine in English in a general intermediate class?

4 Think of some pronunciation difficulties that any one nationality might have with new words; deceptive equivalents of English words in that language; and genuine equivalents.

Exercises

1   Look at any text and decide which words you would want students at various levels to absorb into their active, and which into their passive vocabulary. How would you get them to learn the ones you wish them to be able to use actively?

2   Write out as much common vocabulary as you can which could be used for shopping and shops at early intermediate level, e.g. shop assistants, buy, etc.

3   Work out a plan for teaching vocabulary connected with a street scene on a wall chart for late elementary students. What structures would you revise and how would you blend these with the new words you introduce?

4   Think of ways of presenting and explaining the following words:
considerate   hurry   propellor   meteorite
sympathy   announce   ditch   nourish
regret   pronounce   whale

6 Teaching pronunciation

Pronunciation is probably the most neglected aspect of English language teaching. Foreign teachers often lack confidence to teach it methodically and English teachers sometimes have a complex about it. As with English grammar, applied phonetics is rarely taught at school or even university, and therefore seems an alien, abstract subject to the adult trainee teacher. Then there is the fact that many native English speakers find it difficult to hear certain features such as the fall or rise of speech, particularly at the end of a sentence. The reaction to this is often: 'Well, I'm an educated English person and if I can't detect things like that, the foreign student won't be able to. So what does it matter anyway?

Most pronunciation teaching, as a result, tends to concentrate on individual sounds, which although the most obvious, is not necessarily the most important part.

The teaching of pronunciation should, however, be an integral part of any course. For one thing, students are as concerned about it as they are with any aspect of learning English. In a survey of 500 adult students from Cordoba, Barcelona, Paris, Turin and Rome conducted in 1973, one of the questions asked was 'What do you find most difficult in English: "Grammar", "Speaking", "Understanding", "Pronunciation", "Idioms", "Writing"?' Among these alternatives 'Pronunciation' was in a substantial majority.

Skilled pronunciation teaching also gives life to a class because it reflects feeling and personal reactions to different situations. In classroom practice, it gives variety to repetition or dialogues which, otherwise, have only a neutral meaning.

As mentioned earlier, the meaning of 'Yes' depends on whether it is Yes, or Yes or Yes or Yes. It can even have a meaning that is as close to the negative as to the positive form: Yes.

One argument that the unversed teacher has against pronunciation teaching is that it varies so much, depending on the situation and mood of the speaker, that it seems impossible to standardise anything. This argument, however, could also apply to grammar, as structure also depends on what the speaker is trying to say. Nevertheless, it is possible to make some attempt to break up English grammar into general rules and formulae. In the same way it is possible to lay down general guidelines for English pronunciation. The outline below is an attempt to do this. It is extremely simple because it is only a starting-point. Once the teacher has grasped it, he can extend his knowledge by further reading and by classroom practice. Let us look, then, at various basic elements of English

55

pronunciation which are relevant to effective classroom teaching. Please say all the examples out loud.

6.1. Static forms

These consist of elements which have to be practised individually to ensure intelligibility.

6.1.1. Word stress

Fortunately, the primary stress in most English words is on the first syllable:

Window, market, London, beautiful, manage, hospital, country.

This also applies to genuine compounds:

bookshop, post-office, sitting-room.

Prefixes are not usually stressed:

reply, prepare, begin, understand.

With words of more than three syllables, the stress is often on the spoken syllable that is third from the end:

Philosophy, laboratory, kilometre, psychological.

A few types of words, like those ending in *-tion* and many ending in *-ic* are stressed on the second from the end, while words borrowed recently from other languages often have the stress on the last syllable.

guarantee, cigarette, magazine, hotel, address, shampoo.

6.1.2. Sounds

If other aspects of pronunciation are dealt with efficiently, sounds do not present such a problem. Again, much of the difficulty which students have when pronouncing English sounds comes, not from a physical inability to form them, but from language interference. This occurs when the student knows how an English word is spelt and pronounces it as if it were written in his own language. Thus a German is capable of pronouncing both *w* as in 'women' and *v* as in 'vine' but he confuses them in English, largely because *w* is pronounced like our *v* in his language.

Nevertheless, it is important for a teacher to know how sounds are formed so that he understands what his students are doing wrong.

The drawing on page 57 shows the most important parts in the mouth for the production of sounds.

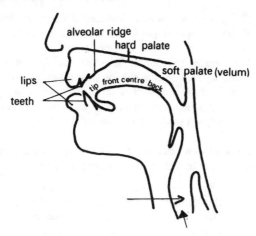

6.1.3. Consonants

The following classification of sounds follows from a description of what the mouth is doing when they are produced.

Bi-labial: When the airstream pushes open the closed lips to form a consonant like *p* in 'pet'.

Dental: When the airstream pushes past tongue tip, placed against or between the teeth to form a consonant like *th* in 'three'.

Alveolar: When the airstream pushes open a closure between the tongue tip and the teeth ridge to form consonants like *t* in 'time'. .

Palatal: When the airstream filters through between the raised centre of the tongue and the palate as with *y* in 'yet'.

Velar: When the airstream pushes open a closure between the back of the tongue and the soft palate (or velum) as with *k* in 'kick'.

Consonants vary depending on where and how the airstream gets through, the place and movement of the tongue, and also whether the voice is used or not. With some consonants, like *w*, *r* and *sh*, the positioning of the lips is involved too. From this come various terms:

Voiced
Voiceless: } These describe whether the voice is used, (i.e. whether the vocal cords vibrate) as it is in *v* in 'vine', or whether it is not, as in *f* in 'fine'. (Try saying *f* then *v* with your finger over your vocal cords. You can feel the difference.)

Plosive: Certain consonants are formed by blocking the air stream and then releasing it suddenly. e.g. with the back of the tongue as in /k/, /g/, with the tongue tip as in /t/, /d/, or with the lips as in /p/ and /b/.

Affricate: Here, the airstream is blocked and then released slowly, as in /tʃ/ and voiced partner /dʒ/ 'chain', 'Jane'.

Fricative: This describes a sound produced through the friction of the
                 air stream against partial obstructions in various parts of the
                 mouth, as in *s* in 'slim' or *th* in 'three'.

Nasal: This applies to consonants which are formed with the soft
                 palate lowered so that the air stream passes through the nose:
                 m as in 'mat', *n* as in 'not', and /ŋ/ as in 'song'.

Lateral: The only lateral consonant is *l*, as in 'long', so-called because
                 the airstream passes at the side of the tongue.

The interrelation between voice, or absence of voice, and the way the mouth
is formed and moves, can be seen in the following examples:

Consonant		Place	Manner	Voice
ʃ	far	labio dental	fricative	voiceless
k	kick	velar	plosive	voiceless
d	do	alveolar	plosive	voiced
ng	song	velar	nasal	voiced
y	yet	palatal	semi vowel	voiced

Try pronouncing these consonants, noticing how they are formed. Then do
the same with other consonants and see if you can determine what you are doing
to produce them.

Awareness of this is useful as many mistakes made by learners are due to slight
differences in sound production. Thus the Italian tendency to say 'zmile' instead
of 'smile' is because the Italian *s* is voiced before a voiced consonant. Finns on
the other hand tend to say 'I've kot' instead of 'I've got' because *g* cannot begin
a word in their language. One of the characteristics of Indian, as opposed to
British English, is the tendency to curl the tongue tip for /t/ and /d/. When your
students make mistakes, it will help if you can analyse what you, yourself, are
doing when you form consonants.

6.1.4. Vowels

Vowels are always voiced. They are formed in a less noticeable way than
consonants, mainly by the position of the tongue and, secondarily, by the shape
of the lips and movement of the jaw. Different vowels are determined by how
high the tongue is raised in the mouth and by whether it is the front, middle or
back part of the tongue which is being used.

Make the sound *ee* as in 'leek'. Notice that you are raising the front part of
the tongue fairly near the palate. Then make the sound *ar* as in 'lark'. Notice
that you are now raising the back part of the tongue only very slightly.

English vowels are short or long, e.g. 'ship' and 'sheep'. The shape of the lips is
also a determinant. Watch your mouth in a mirror and say *ee*, then change to
o as in 'robe', and *oo* as in 'boot'. Notice how your lips become more rounded.
Look at the following table, pronounce the vowels, and notice how they are
formed in your mouth.

Vowel	Tongue-level	Part of tongue	Length	Lips
'back'	low	front	shortish	spread
'birk'	half-raised	central	long	unrounded
'beck'	half-raised	front	short	unrounded
'boot'	high	back	long	rounded
'book'	less high	central-back	short	slightly rounded

Now try out other vowels and see whether you can determine what differentiates them from one another.

6.1.5. Diphthongs

Students of English tend to elongate or shorten diphthongs. Thus, Germans tend to extend the pronunciation of 'house', as if it were 'Haus' in their own language. In fact, diphthongs should take the same time to pronounce as long vowels, e.g. 'cow' and 'car' should take equally long to say. The French and some other nationalities have no diphthongs at all with the result that a Frenchman will shorten a diphthong and say 'wet' instead of 'wait'.

6.1.6. The phonemic alphabet

You may find it useful to teach advanced students to transcribe passages to the phonemic forms. With beginners, it is worth introducing phonetics for different, difficult sounds or for sound-linking. The phonemic alphabet does simplify the relation between spoken and written English and you, yourself, should know it.

SYMBOLS FOR TRANSCRIBING ENGLISH SOUNDS

	Vowels			*Diphthongs*	
Front	/iː/	bead		/eɪ/	bay
	/ɪ/	bid		/aɪ/	buy
	/e/	bed		/ɔɪ/	boy
	/æ/	bad			
				/aʊ/	how
Back	/ɑː/	card		/əʊ/	no
	/ɒ/	cod			
	/ɔː/	cord		/ɪə/	beer
	/ʊ/	good		/ɛə/	bear
	/uː/	food		/ʊə/	tour
Central	/ʌ/	bud		(*Syllabic consonants*)	
	/ɜː/	bird		/l̩/	meta<u>l</u>
	/ə/	cupb<u>oar</u>d		/n̩/	baco<u>n</u>)

Consonants

/p/	pop	/f/	fifteen	/m/	marmalade
/b/	Bob	/v/	vivid	/n/	nine
/t/	tart	/θ/	thirteenth	/ŋ/	singing
/d/	did	/ð/	those	/l/	lip
/k/	cake	/s/	bus	/ł/	pill
/g/	gag	/z/	buzz	/r/	rose
		/ʃ/	cash	/j/	yes
/tʃ/	church	/ʒ/	casual	/w/	way
/dʒ/	judge			/h/	hello

6.1.7. Word-linking

One of the problems of pronunciation is that the foreign learner is reluctant to let words run into one another. Without good word-linking and good stress, words become unmanageable chunks, and fluency is obstructed.

She isn't tall.   He's singing.   No, I'm a student.

6.2. Expressive forms

These consist of elements whose fluctuations have to be shown if the speaker wants to make his intention and feelings clear.

6.2.1. Sentence stress

This distinguishes words which the speaker regards as most important in a sentence.

> A: Do you speak **French**?
> B: Yes. Do **you**?
> A: I can't **speak** it but I can **read** it.

In A's question, **French** is the most important part of the sentence because this is the basic issue that is being discussed. In B's question, however, it is already known which subject is being referred to, and the important question is whether YOU speak it too. In A's answer, the important thing is to distinguish between what A can do and what he can't do, so **speak** and **read** are stressed.

Stress varies according to what the speaker wants to say. Look at the following:

> This is a German **book** – emphasising that it is a book rather than anything else.
>
> This is a **German** book – emphasising that it is German rather than French or any other nationality.
>
> **This** is a German book – emphasising that this object, rather than another one, is a German book.
>
> This **is** a German book – it really is a German book – not something else.

Main stress, therefore, changes as the speaker's intention or the context itself changes, emphasising, for instance, new information:

'Look at that **hotel**.'
'It's a **big** hotel.'
'It's an **expensive** hotel.'

These are all very simple examples but once you have become aware of stress, the logic holds even in complicated sentences with more than one stress.

6.2.2. Unstressed syllables and words — Weak forms

When we say vowels aloud in isolation, we stress each of them: *a, e, i, o, u*. However, as only certain parts of a word or sentence are stressed the remainder are often pronounced in a different way. Thus, these vowels would not be pronounced as they are above if they were part of a word or sentence which was not stressed. Try reading these aloud: '**dra**ma/dra**matic**'; '**his**tory/his**tor**ical'. Then these sentences:

'I **was** here yesterday.'
'I was **here** yesterday.'

Here, 'was' in the first sentence is pronounced differently from 'was' in the second sentence.

Stress, then, produces natural differences in pronunciation. If you teach stress, the weak forms will fall into place without too much difficulty. If you don't, your students will fail not only to convey what they mean, but also to use weak forms.

6.2.3. Voice range

This is the way the voice moves from a high to low pitch or vice versa. Excitement uses a wider voice range, while any feeling that is subdued, sad, indifferent or bored is shown by an absence of variations.

'Oh.' (How terrible)
'Oh.' (How dull)

Note the contrasts:

'I've lost my matches.'
'I've lost my cigarettes.'
'I've lost my lighter!'

If the speaker is a chain smoker and buys very expensive cigarettes and has a very cheap lighter, the voice range of the second and third sentences might be reversed. Voice range, then, is a personal instrument with which any speaker of English can express the strength of his feelings in a situation. It usually comes into operation on the first stressed word in a sentence.

6.2.4. Longer sentences

In longer sentences with several stresses, students have difficulty keeping up the steady rhythm and intonation needed for factual and descriptive utterances. In most of these, the voice tends to move up a greater or lesser extent on the first stressed syllable, descend a little on each stress and fall on the last stress.

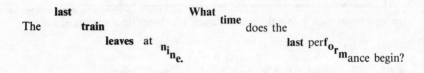

6.2.5. Intonation patterns

These are mainly concerned with the ways in which the voice rises or falls throughout in a sentence. They are more complex because they not only reflect the speaker's mood but also depend on who he is talking to, and the situation in which he finds himself.

However, amidst all these variations it is also possible to determine general rules. Thus, if the speaker is definite and confident, his sentence falls in statements.

1   That's mine!   That's m$_\text{i}$n$_\text{e!}$

2   Eat it!   E$_\text{a}$t it!

3   It's yellow.   It's y$_\text{e}$l low.

This confidence, or definiteness, may be tempered by certain considerations related to the situation, or the person spoken to, and the sentence rises. Examples of these considerations are uncertainty, politeness, concern, and pausing.

1   That's mine!   That's$_\text{m}$i ne.

2   Eat it!   Ea$^\text{t}$ it!

3   It's yellow.   It's$_\text{yel}$low

Questions with yes–no answers often rise or fall-rise at the end. Notice that they tend to start fairly high in polite and interested questions.

1 Are you coming?

Are you $_{co}m^{ing?}$

2 Is he ill?

Is he $_{i}l^{l?}$

3 Do you like chocolate?

Do you **like** $_{ch_{o}c}$olate?

A question beginning with 'Who', 'What', 'Where', 'Why' or 'How many?', however, is often heard to fall at the end:

1 Who's that lady on the left?

Who's that $_{lady on the}l_{e}f_{t?}$

2 What's that lever for?

What's that $_{l}e_{ver for?}$

3 Why do they close at lunch-time?

Why do they $_{close at}l_{un}c_{h}$-time?

4 How many eggs are there?

How many $_{e}g_{g}s$ are there?

Of course, if he wants to sound more gentle, he may temper these questions with a rise or a fall-rise at the end.

1 **Who's** that $_{lady on the}{}_{le}f^{t?}$

2 **What's** that $_{le}v^{e}{}^{r for?}$

3 **Why** do they $_{close at}l_{un}c_{h}$- time?

4 How many $^{e}g_{g}s$ are there?

6.2.6. Tone and tempo

Mood and attitude are also expressed by saying things lightly or gruffly and by whether they are said fast or slowly. This is similar in most languages.

6.2.7. Fluency

The 'static' elements in pronunciation: sounds, word-stress, and word-linking have to be polished and developed individually. The 'expressive' elements, on the other hand, are used according to what the speaker feels or wants to say: he pulls out the different stops on the organ according to the music he is playing, using voice range, sentence stress, intonation patterns, tone, or all of these together, to attain fluency and precision of expression. Let us take some examples, using the simple question, 'What time is it?'

(a) In a straightforward situation, you would have neither a narrow nor a wide voice range. You would stress 'time' because this is what you want to know. Unless you are being very polite or exuberant, the intonation falls:

$$\text{What } t_{i}m_{e} \text{ is it?}$$

(b) On the other hand, you may have your mind on something else or you may just feel casual. There is no need for a wide voice range so you keep it narrow.

$$\text{What } {}^{t}i\text{me is it?}$$

(c) You're very sorry to bother the person you are asking. You show interest which justifies your asking the question: therefore the voice range is wide. To make it more polite you introduce a rise. Your tone is gentle.

$$\text{What}_{\ \ t}i\text{m}^{e}\text{ is it?}$$

(d) You can't believe your ears that it is so late. Because you are surprised, you extend your voice range. As you are doubtful, you put the stress on the question word 'What?' As you don't believe the answer, you are doubtful, so the question ends with a rise.

$$_{Wh}a^{t}\text{ time is }^{it}?$$

In all these sentences, the foreign learner would have to ensure that his pronunciation of the sounds was correct. He would have to make sure of sound-linking. He would also have to make sure that most vowels except the stressed ones were pronounced weakly. By bringing all these things together, he should be speaking more like a 'native' and, at the same time, giving the particular significance he wants to the question.

6.2.8. Summary

If you are not sure whether sentences are rising or falling and you cannot detect the correct stress, don't be dismayed. Ideally, you should take a short course in ear training. If this is impossible, one of the best ways is to listen to reading passages or dialogues on a tape, and go over them carefully, analysing the way language is behaving. If in doubt, you should be able to work out the stresses, and the rises and falls by the sense of the passage, the situations and the intentions of the speaker. In this way, you will acquire confidence and gradually make yourself more sensitive to the rhythm of the language. Also, listen to what is said around you, examine what you say yourself, and try to sort out the general principles outlined above. Remember, however, that this is a general outline. So, once you have grasped it, read further for more details, examples and variations. You will find that being aware of English pronunciation becomes a part of you, rather than appearing to be a mass of general principles which you have difficulty in remembering. Your students go through the same process when they learn English: they apprehend what you teach them, and only when they practise it and apply it for some time does it become easy to use.

6.3. Application in class

Ideally the teacher should present and practise new pronunciation points as he introduces other aspects of language. Thus, if a teacher begins his course with 'I'm' and 'It's' in order to get his beginners to identify themselves in English, so should he introduce stress, intonation, voice range and word-linking right at the start:

'I'm It^{al}ian.'

'It's a ^{let}ter.'

When the pronunciation of simple statements is familiar, the class goes on to questions:

'Are you $_{Span}$ish?'

'Is it from A- ica?'
$_{mer}$

As the teacher gives exercises in structure and vocabulary, he should also help and encourage the students to apply the pronunciation points he has taught. Teachers may feel that this slows the tempo of a class. However, once the students grasp the elements of pronunciation, they advance faster with spoken English and they have greater insight into the language. Lessons are more lively, and structure and vocabulary are also revised more effectively, as they are practised indirectly.

The following suggestions are samples of the kind of presentation that is possible.

6.3.1. Sounds

Some sounds will give students more trouble than others, such as *th*, *o*, final *-s*, *-t* and *-d*, as well as the novel /ɜː/ as in '*first*'. It seems to help them considerably, however, if you keep a poster of the phonemic alphabet on the wall, to enable you to spell any difficult words phonemically for them.

Several consonants together, as in '*str*ing' or '*expect*' often prove difficult, too. Given a little sympathy and time to get their tongues round them, most learners will tackle them.

Word-linking also removes some mispronunciations, like the unwanted *h*: 'No I'm not' instead of No − h − I'm not. 'Yes, you are', 'In it' and so on.

Develop strategies for improvement similar to those which are exemplified below with the consonant *th* as in 'three' and in 'this' and with the dipthong *o* as in 'boat' − which students of all nationalities mispronounce.

'th'

The mistake usually consists in using a *t* or an *s* or *z*.

So show your students how to say it in a lisping sort of way, pressing the tongue almost through the teeth. Then practise any words, whether known or not with energy: through − three − throw   thief − thigh − thick   bath − both − birth   month − length − width.

Then practise responses which are familiar to your students. These will obviously depend on how much your students know, and the following are only examples. Bring in as much revision of idiom, structure and vocabulary as you think useful.

Situation	*Prompts*	*Students:*
Overbidding for an object	Sums and figures on blackboard	3 − 13 − 23 − 33 30 − 31! − 33!! 300 − 303!
Disagreeing about a date	Dates on blackboard	The 3rd? No, the 4th. No, the 5th.
Finding two people born in the same month		What month/When is your birthday? − September the 15th.
Everyone practising to a rhythm	Words on blackboard	This or that? This one or that one? With or without? Here and there. The one with spots or the one with stripes?

You can of course introduce exercises like these at an appropriate time during your lesson using material you think is useful. Or you may want to practise a little and then come back to it later on. You could also develop appropriate dialogues or situations.

As an example, bring in pens and compare their thicknesses, pretending not to know(!)

A: Are these thicker? (refer to the very thin ones)
B: Those are thicker.
A: Are those thicker?
B: No, those are thinner than these.

Then B asks C and so on round the class.
The more deadpan, the better the practice.

As seen, exercises like these also give lateral practice in stress, weak forms and voice range in certain grammar aspects, too.

Now let us apply this to *o* as in 'don't'.

'o'
This is also difficult for all nationalities, largely because they are not accustomed to bringing their lips together to form the dipthong. So get them to make closing lip movements.

Then practise the sound in isolation.

Go on to genuine or nonsense words: 'tope', 'pope', 'pome', 'phone', 'bone', 'don't', 'no'. Then devise some exchanges:

Situation	Prompt	Response
Disappointed	'Oh no! It's raining.'	'Oh no!'
Angry	'Phone him.'	'No. I won't!'
Inquiring	'Do you know him?'	'No. I don't.'
Pointing	'Is that a Boeing?'	'I don't think so.'
Introducing	'This is Joe.'	'Hello.'

Because 'don't', 'won't', and 'no' are common words, we can also get a large number of variations here with prompts.

Start with a pattern, e.g.:

'Drink this!'   'No, I won't!'/'I don't want to.'

Then suggest variations.

'Drink this!'   'No, I won't.'
'Drink that!'   'No, I don't want to.'
'Drink the water!'
'Drink it!'
'Eat it!'

'Eat the food.'
'Take the food.'
'Take your homework.'
'Do your homework.'
'Do your exercises.'

Then devise an appropriate dialogue. Perhaps two children at a birthday party:

A: Show me your present.
B: No. I won't!
A: Show me! (*grabs it*)
B: Don't! (*takes it back*)
A: Please.
B: No!
A: Why not?
B: Because I don't want to.

Bring in visual aids where you can. When comparing vowels, one approach is to use two sheets of paper with different words on them. For instance, 'hole' and 'hall'. Put the two different pieces of paper on opposite corners of the classroom.

Then pass a student another piece of paper with one of the two words written on it. He then has to tell someone to go to either the 'hall' or the 'hole' and, judging by the consequent movement, you can tell whether pronunciation and comprehension have been accurate.

Once you have established and developed some of these exercises with sounds, correct further mistakes as they are made.

Avoid tongue twisters as they rarely contain useful language and are often difficult, even for English people.

6.3.2. Word stress
One way of demonstrating this is to use large circles for the stressed syllables and small circles for those which are unstressed.

O o   O o o   o O o   o O   o o O
office   restaurant policeman hello   cigarette

To revise and test this, you can write the symbols with examples on the board and get students to list the appropriate words under them:

office, restaurant, Paris,	O o	O o o	o O o	o o O
doctor, policeman, article,	morning	yesterday	tomorrow	afternoon
money, unhappy, speaking,				
magazine.				

6.3.3. Word-linking

Make students aware of this at the beginning:

I'm an engineer.   What time is it?   He's speaking.   My address.

Encourage this throughout the students' speech, as it improves their fluency. Pick out any good examples on tapes played. Dictate sound-linked phrases. Then get the students to read them back to you, so that you make them aware of the way sounds can be assimilated. Create responses and dialogues, which practise specific sound-linking, e.g.

A: Where's New York?   A: What is she doing?   A: She's got a lot of
                                                       money.

B: In America.   B: What does she do?   B: Oh, has she?

A: Where's Lisbon?   A: Yes, she has.

B: In Portugal.

6.3.4. Sentence stress

Demonstrate, right at the beginning, how stress operates by emphasising the most important words in a sentence. There are various ways of indicating stress on the board. A common way is to draw a little square over the stressed syllable(s) or to stick brightly coloured little squares onto the blackboard, using Blu-tack. Then the stress can be moved about, as it does in speech:

    □   □   □   □
The seventh of July;   I'm from Italy. − Oh, I'm from Italy.

One way of accustoming your students to use stress, is to get them to say only the stressed parts of words in a sentence: pausing for the others:

This is a **let**ter from New **York.**
This   **let**   **York.**

When they then fill in the complete sentence, they also become aware of the intervening weak forms.

Alternatives and contrasts are a good way of bringing out stress clearly, because they distinguish the important part of a sentence, e.g.:

'Do you want **tea** or **coff**ee?'
'**I'd** like **tea** but **he** wants **coff**ee.'

Visual aids and objects brought into the classroom can also help here. Bring in two bottles of different sizes:

'It's a **bottle**.'
'It's a **bottle**.'
'It's a **big** bottle.'
'It's a **small** bottle.'

You can elaborate further by having them full or empty, of different colours, etc.

Disagreements and contradictions also emphasise the important words, e.g.:

'Two and two are **five**!'
'Two and two are **four**!'

'Is it the **first** of November?'
'No. It's the **second** of November.'

Help your students get into the habit of stressing what to them are the most important parts of a sentence by showing them how to move stress too:

Is it the second of October?
No, the second of November.

Train them to ask the same question back, at the same time moving the stress, in the normal way:

A: Where are you **from**?

B: From Japan. Where do **you** come from?

A simple way is to get them to ask each other a question with a basic structure, while the teacher prompts with different vocabulary, e.g.:

Prompts	*Question*	*Possible Answer*
A What are you doing?	What are you **do**ing?	**Stud**ying.
B You.	What are **you** doing?	**Stud**ying.
C Reading	What are you **read**ing?	My **book**.
D You.	What are **you** reading?	My **book**.
E He	What is **he** reading?	**His** book.
	etc.	

As these questions follow one another round the class, they accustom students to the idea that stress shifts to the new information, focus, or person talked to.

Another way is to contrast coloured objects, presenting them one by one:

That's a **blue pen**.
That's a **red** pen.
That's a red **book**.
That's a **blue** book.
etc.

Devise as many exercises as you can, adapted to the structure, vocabulary or idiom you are introducing, or want to revise.

6.3.5. Weak forms

The first weak forms to be taught are probably 'am' and 'is' as in 'I'*m* a student.' and 'What'*s* that?', compared to their 'strong' forms in answers like 'I am.' and 'It is.' Students take a long time adopting the weak, contracted form and need constant reminding to do so. Good use of stress and word-linking will enable the students to speak more rapidly, in turn contracting the intervening little grammar words.

A way of practising them specially is to have the students respond genuinely: E.g.

What do you think it'll be like tomorrow?
I'm sure it'll rain.
I think it'll be colder.
I think it'll be warmer.

Another way of concentrating on weak forms is to write up tables on the board, and point out the word you want stressed, so that the others are pronounced as weak forms, e.g.

A   Look at { me. / him. / them. }   B { He / She / John } was there.   C It's { your } book. / { her } / our } paper. / their }

Take example A: the teacher points at 'Look' and gets the sentence '**look** at me.', then at 'him' and gets the sentence 'Look at **him**.', and so on.

6.3.6. Longer sentences

A useful exercise here which is also good for fluency is to get your students to read and say instructions or factual statements and questions which get longer and longer, e.g.:

'**Turn**.'
'**Turn left**.'
'**Turn left** at the **end**.'
'**Turn left** at the **end** of the **street**.'

6.3.7. Expression – voice range and intonation

It is difficult to separate the different elements, here, as they are closely inter-related. The essential thing is to get your students aware that they will learn more naturally and rapidly if they are expressive. Show them how to manipulate voice range and intonation so that they can reflect their certainties or doubts, their statements or questions, and their moods and attitudes.

Make students sound definite when stating facts, as this helps their voices fall:

'It's $T_{u_{e_{s}}}$day.'   'She's in $L_{o_{n}}$don.'   '**Someone's** $k_{n_{o_{c_{k}}}}$ing.'

When introducing questions, the crucial issue will be the students' ability to ask a question politely, as unpleasantness is likely to result if he can't. One way of introducing and practising this is to get a student to ask a favour politely rather than without interest:

'Could you lend me £5/your car/some money/your bicycle, please?'
'Can I have a cigarette/a light/a match/a beer, please?'
'Would you open/close the window/door, please?'
'Could you speak/talk more slowly, please?'
etc.

The student who is addressed has to decide whether the request was pleasant enough for him to accede to it, thus testing his own comprehension and the questioner's politeness, or lack of it.

Introducing contrasts in voice range at all levels, or in combination with other teaching, stimulates expressiveness, especially with the aid of mood cards, one

with a cheerful face on it ☺ and another with a glum expression ☹ .

Simply show your class one or the other of these when you want your students to speak, whether in drills or dialogues.

You can show what you mean by voice range on the board:

Wide ⌐̲̅   Narrow ⫤

Get them making statements which by their nature involve a wide or narrow voice range:

I'm tired. ⟋   I'm so happy! ⟍

It's wonderful! ⟍   It's all right. ⟋

Get them to react with a simple response like 'Really':

You've won £100.   re̶ally?!

It's raining. $\overline{\text{re}}$
                 $\underline{\quad\text{ally.}\quad}$

Tomorrow's a holiday. $\overline{\text{re}}$
                         $\underline{\quad\text{al}^{\text{ly.}}\quad}$

Matches are made of wood, you see. $\overline{\quad_{\text{re}}^{\text{ally?}}\quad}$
                                      $\underline{\qquad\qquad}$

Or with gratitude for a gift: put a match, a safety pin and other insignificant objects in separate envelopes. Write 'A Rolls Royce', '£5 for you!' etc. on pieces of paper and do likewise. Distribute the envelopes and get the students to thank you with a wide or narrow voice range, according to their appreciation.

A simple way of making the student aware of both falls and rises is to practise offers and answers — without verbs:

Tea or coffee?
↗   ↘
Coffee, please.
↘
Milk?
↗
Please.
↘
Sugar?
↗
One or Two?
↗   ↘
etc.

With any enumeration, rises occur until the final item is mentioned. Show this with counting:

One – two – three – four – five.

Get the students to read out English addresses:

Flat 4,
12, Kensington Place,
Kensington Road,
London S.W.5.

There are, of course, many other exercises for simple intonation and voice range which you can devise along these, or other lines. Beyond this, you should have little difficulty in getting students to express definite emotion in English as they get involved, or to imitate. It is valuable, though, to practise certain useful moods and attitudes because it makes them aware of the importance of voice-range and modulation in English and trains them to be expressive. As an example of this, let us take two common emotional attitudes: Arguing and Incredulity.

DISAGREEING

This is often expressed with a fall on 'NO' or 'YES' and a rise at the end of the response. Get your students to state fairly unlikely facts, which other students contradict:

'You know Greenland, don't you?'   'No, I don't'

'But you've been to Greenland.'   'No, I haven't!'

'You were there last year.'   'No, I wasn't!'

INCREDULITY

This can be expressed by repeating the incredible words with a very low rise, or fall-rise. Get your students to make incredible statements, to which others react:

'Cigarettes are now made of potatoes.'   'Potatoes!!?'

'Yes, they cost 5 pence each.'   'Five pence each??'

'Well, you can buy second-hand ones.'   'Second hand ones??!!'

Where moods and attitudes are concerned there are, of course, many variations. However, the more you can get your students interested in this, the more interested they will be in English as a musical instrument rather than as notation. If you pursue this, your more advanced students will also begin to notice variations in the way English people talk, and so will learn in this way.

Further reading

1   Gimson, A.C., *An Introduction to the Pronunciation of English*, Arnold, 1976.

2   Roach, P., *English Phonetics, Phonology*, CUP, 1983.

3   O'Connor, J.D., *Better English Pronunciation*, CUP, 1980.

4   Haycraft, B. and Lee, W.R., *It Depends How You Say It*, Pergammon, 1982.

5   Thompson, I., *Intonation Practice*, OUP, 1981.

6   Baker, A., *Three or Tree?*, CUP, 1982.

7   Baker, A., *Introducing English Pronunciation*, CUP, 1982.

8   Mortimer, C., *Elements of Pronunciation*, CUP, 1985.

Discussion

1   Do you think English teachers are reluctant to teach pronunciation? If so, what are the reasons for this?

2   What does a wide voice range convey?

3   Think of ways to practise the past tense-ending 'ed' in sentences, bearing word-linking in mind, too.

4   Devise short dialogues to practise weak forms at intermediate level.

Exercises

1   Work out how you form the following sounds in your mouth:
     s (bus), *z* (buzz), *r* (roll), *l* (roll), *ee* (peep), *i* (pip).
     How would you help students who have difficulties with these sounds?

2   How many ways can this sentence be said?
     'He can read English very well.'
     Explain how the variations of stress and intonation alter the meaning.

3   Write out as many intonation signs as you can think of for 'No' with the different implications of each.

4   Devise four or five different prompts which would *each* make the stress change in a given sentence of your own choosing.

5   Work out a common intonation and stress pattern for requesting, and then devise an exercise for class practice at intermediate level.

7 Listening practice

Listening, understanding, and responding in an appropriate way is an essential part of communication and, therefore, regular practice in aural comprehension is a vital part of the teaching programme. If most of our classroom time is devoted to oral work, then listening is being practised a great deal of the time. However, there are specific listening activities that càn be included in the syllabus.

7.1. Distinguishing between key sounds, stress, and intonation patterns

Ear-training with spoken practice is essential to building up students' pronunciation. The problem is how to do it briefly yet effectively. Small but vital differences between troublesome sounds can be spotted by letting the students listen and say if they hear number 1 or 2. E.g.

1 Miss Parker
2 Miss Barker

1 Do you like Coke?
2 Would you like a Coke?

1 There are two.
2 They are two.

Intonation can also assist the students' comprehension. By listening to the attitude expressed, like excitement, routine, or impatience, they experience the language more fully. A most rewarding exercise is to have the students predict the likely attitude and the stresses in a dialogue about to be played.

7.2. Quick questions

One aim of the listening comprehension programme must be to train students to understand and respond quickly to the sort of language they are likely to encounter in normal use – in the sort of situations they are likely to find themselves in. The need for situational work – asking for information in shops, in restaurants and so on has been mentioned elsewhere. Apart from this systematic practice, now and again ask your class simple questions in English as fast as you can: 'Who are you?', 'What's your name?', 'What time is it?', 'What's the capital of England?', 'What's two and two?', etc. The object is to train your students to listen with concentration and accustom them to English spoken fast, which is most of the time – except in the average classroom. This is invaluable if done regularly as part of revision, perhaps at the beginning or end of a class. It's surprising how soon this kind of practice can improve your students' concentration and powers of deduction.

7.3. Comprehension passages

Remember that you are training your students to understand English from any part of the world. Get, therefore as much variety of accent in your listening comprehensions. A few years ago it was difficult to get hold of passages with anything but received pronunciation. Now, however, a much wider range is available.

As always you must ask yourself why you are using a particular approach. Is it so that your students can acquire new vocabulary and idiom, to revise language already known, to train them to grasp ideas expressed in English, or descriptions, or for other reasons? Your technique will depend on your objective. Thus you can choose a passage without much new vocabulary, play it only once and give your students practice in grasping the meaning of familiar English, but spoken fast and naturally. Or, choose a piece with unfamiliar words and expressions. Play it several times, allowing your students to deduce the general meaning. Vary your approach. On one occasion you may decide to pre-teach unfamiliar language and on another to encourage your students to use their ability to decipher language.

Remember that it will take time before your class gets used to listening in this way. To begin with, they will say it is too fast. However, if you persevere, they will find it as easy or as difficult as the English really is.

The following is a possible sequence for a piece with new vocabulary and idiom. You may only want to use part of it, or vary it in your own way. Don't spend too long on one stage as all the phases are complementary.

(a) Start by playing the passage as often as you think fit. Ask general questions.

(b) Get the students to repeat sentence by sentence. Introduce new vocabulary related to the situation.

(c) Play parts of the passage and ask more specific questions at times provoking contradiction.

(d) Play it right through and ask more questions.

(e) Distribute the written passage and let your class look at it, while the tape is played. Further questions.

(f) Clear up doubts about structure, idiom, vocabulary and spelling.

(g) Dictation of part of the passage: or of a combination of different parts of it.

(h) Homework. Get students summarising or answering questions, or write a composition inspired by the passage.

7.4. Broadcasts

Part of learning a language is acquiring the ability to listen to radio broadcasts, which are valuable for useful, everyday specialisations such as the news or weather forecasts. Also for highly specialised talks which you can get hold of nowhere else, such as technical, economic or literary discussions. Plays, stories, extracts from novels can also be recorded and used as long as the tapes are not sold commercially. Broadcasts are particularly useful to illustrate intonation and register: compare for instance the difference between the news and a weather forecast.

It is important that you choose the broadcasts yourself to accord with the level of your class, the interrelation with what else you are teaching and your immediate objectives.

7.5. Lectures

These can be valuable at intermediate stage and beyond if they train students in listening, memorising, summarising, asking or answering questions in front of an audience, and in note-taking. They are a useful preparation for university courses and conferences in English. However, it is important to break up monologues in order to fulfil different purposes. Here are suggestions for an approach which can be varied or adapted, depending on your audience and on what you are talking about.

(a) If necessary, train your students how to take notes. Practise dividing material up with headlines, abbreviating words and sentences, and summarising ideas or facts.

(b) Talk about the facts on which your lecture is based for about five to ten minutes. Speak at a normal speed but as clearly as possible. Either adapt your English to the level of the group, or give them practice in grasping the general sense. The more unfamiliar the subject, the simpler the language. Make sure the class take notes.

(c) Ask them questions on what you have talked about. First ask the whole group and then ask individuals.

(d) Go on to the second part of your lecture: talk about ideas related to the facts you have already presented. Enumerate them clearly, with different interpretations and with arguments for and against.

(e) Again, ask the audience questions on what you have just said. Here you are training them to express abstract concepts, neatly and concisely. You are not, however, asking them for their opinions at this stage.

(f) Now that everyone is conversant with the different ideas and possible arguments, get them to put forward their own opinions. Your lecture can then develop into a general discussion. Encourage as many people to speak as possible. This is important because the ability to speak clearly in front of a lot of people, despite nervousness, is an important and useful professional skill, particularly as so many conferences are in English.

To apply this to a specific subject, let us take a lecture on the police in England. In the first ten minutes you might talk about the origins of the Metropolitan Police in 1829, why they are called 'Bobbies', the foundation of the county constabulary in 1840, the way both the Metropolitan Police and the county constabulary are organised. Vary your monologue by asking relevant questions. Thus, if you mention that the City of London Police are separately organised, you could ask someone to describe the difference between the City of London, and the Boroughs, and the City of Westminster.

When you have given all the facts, ask questions; and when you are sure that all the details are clear, you go on to talk about more abstract questions: whether the police should be armed, the relation of corruption to pay, whether a weak, unarmed police force doesn't mean calling on the army in eventualities such as Northern Ireland, etc. When you have finished, ask further questions on what you have said and then have a discussion. Finally, for homework, get everyone to write out their notes clearly, or write a composition on some aspect of the police.

In this way, you have given information about the social background of the language you are teaching, and got students to talk and to listen, while practising a number of other useful language functions.

7.6. Dictations

Some teachers reject dictations as old-fashioned. In fact, teaching English should include the best of 'old-fashioned' techniques applied in a modern and effective way. Dictations are valuable, like written substitution tables, as a bridge between spoken and written English, helping students to consolidate written structures, idiom and vocabulary, which can already be pronounced correctly, and are also a useful test of listening comprehension.

The simplest form consists of short sentences containing elements which a teacher wants to revise. If the aim is consolidation, it is inadvisable to introduce new words. However, at more advanced stages, it may be worth giving them new vocabulary to see if they can work out the spelling from rules they already know.

Ask yourself what material is useful and *likely* to be dictated: telegrams, notes, a business letter to a secretary, telephone numbers, messages, instructions.

Dictation is also comprehension practice and should, therefore, be read at a normal speed, with normal expression. It can then be used to revise speech forms with students recognising sound-linking, word stress and weak forms. It is also a simple way of consolidating or teaching punctuation.

If you give a long dictation, choose a text which is available to everyone afterwards for correction. Students can then correct each other's dictation, which is a useful variation to correcting their own. Otherwise time is wasted writing up long screeds on the blackboard.

Read the dictation as many times as necessary. If you read it fast the first time, you are giving good general comprehension practice. Then read it sentence by sentence as the students write. When you read it through again, you train your students to correct themselves.

Thus, dictations can be used for a number of different skills. You can concentrate on structures you have just taught; you can leave blanks which the students have to fill in. You can dictate the punctuation, or leave it out and get the class to devise it. Alternatively, get one of your students to read the dictation, thus making the whole class aware of the importance of clear dictation. Use dictation in any other way you find useful: merge it with discussion of a text, or reading practice, or reproduction from memory, or the first stage of a composition, or practice in dialogue writing, or the introduction of a passage for précis. Whatever you do, don't simply use it as an automatic exercise to be done two or three times a month, merely because it is part of a conventional syllabus.

An interesting form of dictation suggested by James Duke is getting students to draw what you dictate. They then have to look at the pictures they have drawn and describe them, or answer questions. Obviously, your description has to be entirely visual and simple, so that even the clumsiest can draw it intelligibly. Here is an example for elementary students:

'There is an island in the middle of a lake. In the middle of the island there's a house with a big door and four windows on the ground floor, and six windows on the first floor. There are a lot of big trees to the left of the house. On the lake, to the right of the island, there's a boat with two men in it. One of them is fishing.

To the left of the lake there is a hill with a church on the top. It's midday and the sun is in the sky.'

As can be seen, the main practice in this particular case is with directions; 'to the left/right', 'on the top', 'in the middle', etc. The real advantage, however, is that you are challenging your students to show they understand your description by reproducing it and then describing it themselves.

Further reading

1 Byrne, D., *Teaching Oral English*, Longman, 1986. Chapter 3.

2 Urr, P., *Teaching Listening Comprehension*, CUP, 1982.

Discussion

1 What would determine your choice of a comprehension passage? What would be the advantages of having it on tape?

2 What are the advantages and disadvantages of using radio broadcasts?

3 Why are lectures useful?

Exercises

1 Choose a passage for listening comprehension and describe the stages you would go through when using it in class.

2 Write out a picture dictation (connected with clothing) for an intermediate class.

3 Write out some exercises you would use for testing comprehension of key sound, stress and intonation patterns.

8 Speaking practice

After new language items have been presented to the students, it is essential that they practise the language in a variety of ways and really learn to use what they have been taught.

8.1. Maximise student-talking

8.1.1. Pairwork and groupwork

Students practise the new language item in two's or three's, the teacher at a distance ready to assist as necessary. This provides an almost natural situation for exchanges such as questions and answers, suggestions and reactions, opinions and arguments, etc.

8.1.2. Information gaps and the jigsaw principle

An effective way of stimulating the talking is to issue materials with slight differences for each student. The teacher can just stand back and watch the students finding out what's different or missing. Here's an example which shows that it can happen in real life. A and B are trying to arrange a meeting but it isn't easy, judging by their diaries:

	A	B
Mon	Dentist	Free
Tue	Free	Visit to Birmingham
Wed	Afternoon visit	Dentist 11 am
Thur	10.30 Meeting	Free
Fri	Meeting at 2.30	Meeting all morning

8.1.3. The Pyramid

This refers to the class interaction multiplying from two's to four's and so on. Once the pair come to an agreement or complete their inquiry, they go on to check with the pair next to them, the class thus working in quartets. Various changes and challenges in the materials then move them to explore in eight's and then in sixteen's, until eventually the whole class is involved each with everyone.

8.1.4. Find two people in a crowd with something in common
Here, the situation is like a market survey, asking people their opinion or personal information. Each student has a slightly different task. The rush to find two people who for example think idealism is more important than materialism could produce twice as many questions as there are people in the class, in less than two minutes, with everyone taking part.

8.2. Dialogues

You want your class not only to understand dialogues but also to absorb and reproduce what they contain, whether in terms of acting out or improvisation. If you have a large class, you will need to use dialogues with six or seven characters so that you can involve more students at a time. The following is a suggested sequence, using a recorded dialogue, of how to get your class to act out:

(a) Play the tape as many times as necessary for general comprehension. Ask questions.

(b) Play it line by line, getting the whole class to repeat.

(c) Do the same, getting individuals to repeat.

(d) Get as many students as there are characters in the dialogue *up on their feet*, in front of the class. Give them their roles and get them to repeat line by line.

(e) Give out the script and get each group to act out. Go round checking on pronunciation and realistic role playing.

(f) Take the script away and get students to say what they want, allowing improvisation.

(g) Get everyone to learn a part at home, and then act it out the next day from memory. This is ideal for 'Social English', for structured dialogues, and for four line dialogues (see 4.2.9.).

8.3. Chain stories

These are used at intermediate and advanced stages, as they depend on improvisation.

You make a statement and the students supply a new sentence.

'There was a knock on the door. . . .'
'He went to the door and opened it.'
'A man with a gun was standing there.'
'He shut the door quickly.'
'The man with the gun fired at the door.'
etc.

You can adapt this to happenings in the past if these are interesting to your class, and the students have some idea of the background.

'General de Gaulle flew to London in 1940. . . .'
'He established the French Government here.'

You can use it for business classes, getting them to outline economic or commercial developments, or the history of their firm.

In this way, chain stories become a stage in general studies. These stages could be:

1 Giving and eliciting information where necessary.
2 Getting students to recount.
3 Discussion.

Visual aids can help here: get objects, photographs or drawings that relate to your general theme.

In class, it is probably best to limit students to one sentence, and get the narrative moving as fast as possible. Correct gently. From time to time, get students to recall everything that has been said so far.

8.4. Mime stories

You mime out a simple story, or event, and your students have to tell you what is happening in correct English. This focusses the students' attention because they are trying to decipher your actions. You use it essentially for consolidation, and the students should know most of the words and structures you are eliciting. It must be well prepared. Decide which language area you want, and practise the sequence of actions beforehand, making sure that they are clear and unambiguous. As long as you do this, you can use mime stories from the beginner's stage.

When acting out, you can either run through the whole sequence first, and then mime it section by section. Alternatively, you can go straight into it. The former approach makes it easier, as your students already have an idea of the whole sequence. The latter brings more suspense.

From the beginning, you establish the tense and person that you want to use. As you are the only 'actor' it is difficult to bring in the plural. However, you can get a student to mime with you, or indicate another person by reacting as if someone else was there, or moving position. You repeat the mime until someone produces a correct, opposite sentence.

Some teachers find it difficult to invent mime stories. However, don't feel you have to be brilliant. Much of the entertainment lies in the actual movement and in student participation.

Here are a few simple examples. Notice the alternation between Simple Past and Past Continuous tenses:

1 He opened the door. He called the cat. He went outside. He called the cat again. The cat wasn't there. He went back inside. He looked surprised. The cat was inside all the time.
2 I was driving a car. There was another car coming towards me. There was a crash. I opened the door. I argued. I hit the other driver.
3 She was eating. She found something in the food. She called the waiter. She pointed to the food. She took a hair out of the food. She complained. She

listened to the waiter. She took out one of her own hairs. She compared it. They were both the same. She apologised to the waiter.

4 He was flying an aeroplane. He climbed. The engine failed (began to fail). He looked frightened (afraid). He opened the door. He jumped out. He fell. He pulled. The parachute opened.

5 She was standing in a queue. Someone pushed in front of her. She stared at him angrily. She moved in front of him. He looked angrily back at her. She moved in front of him. (You continue this as often as you wish.) The bus arrived. She ran. She nudged the man with her elbow. She jumped on.

Don't feel you have to be a superb actor – any more than when playing charades. Number 5 could involve more complicated mime, as another person is brought in. If you find that kind of story too difficult, don't try it. Follow a simpler action sequence, like Number 2 or 4, which hardly need a Laurence Olivier. In any case, invent something which suits your class and you. You can do something as simple as pretending to open an umbrella, finding it impossible, throwing it angrily away, and then walking on in the rain. For beginners, you could even make it as elementary as eating something and finding the food is bad.

In order to practise the sentences more often, devise signs for repetition. Put your hand on top of your head when you want the previous sentence repeated, or turn it round when you want the whole story repeated from the beginning. Make it clear to your class what these signs mean, beforehand.

Notice that the language in the stories is stilted as it is split up into short sentences. If you want to make it more fluent, devise signs for 'and', 'then', etc.

It might be helpful to imagine one of these stories mimed in the classroom, so let us take Number 2. Notice that this story would be more appropriate in certain countries than in others.

8.4.1. Preparation

You establish that the narrative is in the first person. If they don't know words like 'crash' or 'argue', you introduce them in context. Before the class, you rehearse the mime by yourself and make sure it's as unambiguous as possible.

8.4.2. Mime stages

1 *Mime* You sit down and drive an imaginary car. Then face the class and wait for suggestions.

Suggestions 'I'm a taxi driver.' You shake your head. 'I'm driving.' You indicate that this is almost right. 'I'm driving a car.' You point your thumb over your shoulder to indicate the past. 'I was driving a car.' You put your hand on top of your head. The class repeat 'I was driving a car'.

2 *Mime* You go on driving, then suddenly sit back with a look of alarm.

Suggestions 'There's a dog in the road.' Shake your head. 'I was ill.' Shake your head. 'I was afraid.' Shake your head. Point to where the 'road' is. 'There was a car.' Nod but indicate that you want more guesses. 'There was other car.'

Nod but go to the blackboard and write 'another'. 'There was another car.' Nod but extend a hand and indicate movement towards yourself. 'There was another car coming.' Indicate movement towards yourself again. 'There was another car coming towards me.' Clap your hands. Turn your hand around to indicate repetition from the beginning. The class say: 'I was driving a car! There was another car coming towards me.'

3 *Mime* Put your hand back on the steering wheel. Throw your body about, to indicate the crash.

Suggestions 'A car hit me.' Nod but look uncertain. 'Another car hit you.' Write 'it' on the board. Point to a student who hasn't said anything, holding up your other hand to restrain the rest of the class. 'It hit me.' Although this isn't what you originally planned it is good enough. Clap your hands.

4 *Mime* Open the 'door' of the car.

Suggestions 'I opened the window.' You look perplexed. 'I opened the door.' Clap. Point to a student who hasn't said anything. Whirl your hand about. 'I was driving a car. There was another car coming towards me. It hit me. I opened the door.'

5 *Mime* You 'get out', look at an imaginary person, wave your arms about with your lips moving. Point at the 'front' of your 'car'.

Suggestions 'I got out and shouted.' You realise that in your preparation you've omitted the stage of actually getting out of the car. Luckily however, a student has provided it. You nod your head but still look uncertain. 'I've got out of the car and fought.' Look uncertain and shake your head. 'I got out of the car and discussed.' No. They try a lot of alternatives which are not suitable, so you write 'argued' on the board. One student can't pronounce it properly so you point to your lips to indicate that it is the pronunciation that is wrong. Other students try. When one gets it right, you nod and get the others to repeat it. Then you indicate a student who hasn't spoken yet and he repeats everything from the beginning: 'I was driving a car. There was another car coming towards me. It hit me. I opened the door. I got out and argued.'

Continue.

The above brings out some of the problems that can emerge. Notice the way the board has been used to help out. You can extend this further and use drawing in combination with mime. If you find that the class can't get the right sentence, you can tell it to them, but it is a pity, as they will guess less assiduously because they know they will be given the answer in the end.

The whole process need not take long, and it is effective because it uses parts of the language process which are difficult to practise in other ways. You can extend it by getting a student to do the actual mime. Rehearse it with him beforehand. While he acts it out, you can elicit and correct.

8.5. Telling jokes

This is difficult in any language, and yet it is an essential part of conversation and personal communication. Although most textbooks have elements of humour, there are few which actually encourage students to produce it themselves.

One obvious approach is to get each student to think of a joke, prepare it for homework, rehearse it by him/herself and then tell it in class. It is essential to ensure fluency and verve, and to emphasise the importance of leading up to the climax with the right stress and intonation. It doesn't matter particularly whether the rest of the class have heard the story before. It is important to give a lot of encouragement and minimise the jeers that result from a bad, or badly told, joke.

Let us go through one of the many ways of teaching through jokes:

1   Tell the joke:
There was an Italian living in London. One day, he bought a large melon and walked along Piccadilly with it. A man stopped him. 'Excuse me,' he said, 'but can you tell me the way to Trafalgar Square?'

The Italian spoke good English and he knew where Trafalgar Square was, but he just looked at the man, and he couldn't say anything. His lips moved but no words came out, and a look of pain came over his face.

'What's wrong?' asked the other man.

The Italian suddenly held out the melon and the man took it. 'Ah,' said the Italian, smiling and moving his hands, 'you go straight down there to Leicester Square and then turn right down Charing Cross Road.' Now that his hands were free, he could speak.

2   Ask questions: Where was the Italian? Had he bought an apple? Why did a man stop him? etc. Make sure by the end of your questioning that everybody understands.

3   Take the story in sections. Get a student to set the situation; another to describe the Italian's frustration; another to describe what the Italian did; another to reproduce the Italian's directions; another to say the last line. Work on this in terms of natural narrative style, with dramatic climaxes, and the appropriate stress and intonation.

4   Get students to act out the dialogue. Get a large object for one of them to hold, and get a good mimed representation of the Italian's frustration, and the other man's perplexity.

5   Get students telling the whole story with as much skill as possible.

6   Get the students to write out the story for homework.

7   Several days or weeks later, get students telling the whole story from memory with any improvisation they wish, for revision.

I've deliberately chosen a story which teases one nationality to emphasise that you must be careful with jokes or stories you choose. This might conceivably offend a touchy Italian class. Again, it is unlikely to go down with a group of students in Japan because they probably know little about Italians, anyway, and therefore might not see the point. When preparing beforehand, write out your story in the kind of language that your students understand easily. Fluency is the object here, and if there are a lot of unknown words and concepts, the whole exercise will be slow and sticky and difficult. Divide your story up into natural stages and try to bring in as much dialogue as you can for acting out. Record it on tape if possible.

This is bound to be an artificial exercise, but your students can then apply what they have learnt to produce their own stories with greater confidence. However, don't go on interminably, so that they never want to tell a story in English again. As always, the balance is between methodical teaching and student involvement. This requires systematic preparation beforehand, flexibility in the classroom and lightness of touch.

8.6. Talks/lecturettes

These accustom students to giving talks in front of other people. Make sure the subject is one that the speaker knows a lot about. Don't get all your class to prepare lecturettes at the same time, as you will never be able to get through them in the next few periods. Perhaps the best way is to have one student giving a short lecturette every lesson. Make sure they are very short, or they will engulf your timetable. Also use them as a means of teaching remedial English: get other students noting down mistakes while the talk is going on; then discuss them afterwards.

8.7. Conversation

Most classes are designed to practise specific speaking or listening skills. However, there should be times when students can express themselves without any aim in mind except general conversation.

This can begin at an early stage with students chatting about their daily programme, or what they did the previous evening, or where they live, or their last holiday. The subject of conversation has to be chosen carefully within the limits of what the students know.

At intermediate stages, it should be possible to discuss themes. Suggest these and get the class to do the same. Then decide on the one which interests most of them. Preferably, get them to prepare an outline for homework in note form, putting forward the arguments in favour and against, and finally a summary of views. You correct it and when you give it back you engender a discussion.

In this way, you involve them by making them work out their views, so you can encourage argument during the discussion.

At other times, you may find that discussions need no preparation and that they spring up spontaneously. Try to take advantage of this. Remember that you probably teach most when your students really want to say something in English. So adapt your timetable, as long as the subject interests most of the class, but don't get carried away.

In any discussion, your role is normally that of a stimulator. Don't regard these periods simply as opportunities to express views of your own. Throw in ideas if there is a long lull, or you feel that a new idea will provoke more discussion. Make sure that everyone speaks, by asking questions, or by steering the discussion towards people who haven't said anything.

Discussions can be provoked in many ways: by reading a passage, or book, or story, and then discussing it; by going to see a film as a class and then talking about it afterwards; by interpolating the reading of newspapers with discussions on news items; by getting students to deliver lecturettes and then going over what they have said. Very often the best themes are personal but common to everyone: early schooldays, first memories, illness, accidents, friendship; or for adults: first jobs, last exams, criticisms of school/university, ambition, etc.

Insistent correction can hinder expression. However, it is possible to correct almost as an aside. Otherwise, note flagrant mistakes and go over them afterwards.

Don't forget to integrate discussion with other forms of study. Follow up with a composition on the same theme if you feel that your class are still interested in the subject. Or teach relevant vocabulary or idiom before or after, prompting with it, if necessary, during the discussion. Because students need this new language they will absorb it more readily.

8.8. Role playing and improvisation

Acting out dialogue has already been mentioned (see p. 81). Acting in language learning is valuable because we are all, perhaps, actors when speaking another language; because it accustoms students to perform in front of others, which is what they have to do outside the classroom; because it helps them to overcome the nervousness which this entails; because it gets them speaking expressively in a situation, and thus makes them more aware of stress and intonation in speech; because it involves everyone, as those in the 'audience' want to see how their fellow students will perform, conscious that they too will soon be on 'stage' themselves.

It is also possible that we learn a language best when we approach it indirectly. A child does not concentrate on vocabulary, structure, and idiom, but on what it wants, and language emerges as an indirect product of this. In the same way, students concentrating on a role, with movements and stage 'business', will often produce more natural language than those with purely linguistic objectives.

Some teachers feel that acting out is impractical with shy students. In fact, people are often reluctant to speak a foreign language because they are afraid of making a fool of themselves. When acting, however, they can shield their own personalities with the role they are playing.

The real value of acting out is as a first stage towards improvisation, as a memorised dialogue is of doubtful value except on formalised occasions, such as introductions, asking for things in a shop, polite refusals, etc.

In role playing, you have three elements: what the characters want, who they are, and their moods or attitudes at the time. These elements are then affected by how the situation develops.

Thus, at a simple level you could have a man going into a shop to ask for a packet of cigarettes. You extend the dimension by giving roles to customer and shop assistant:

Characters:
Customer   He is a chain smoker and needs a cigarette desperately. He smokes Gauloises. He is aggressive.
Shop-Assistant   She is slightly deaf and it isn't her shop. She doesn't care how much she sells. She is sloppy and apathetic.
Situation: The shop doesn't stock Gauloises. They have other cigarettes.
Mannerisms: The chain smoker coughs a lot. He is nervous. The shop assistant is knitting.
Developments: The customer asks for Gauloises but can't get them. The shop assistant offers him other cigarettes.
Props: The more of these you have the better: packets of different cigarettes, knitting needles, a 'counter'.

You may not be able to explain all this as your students are unlikely to be advanced enough. However, you can convey deafness, produce knitting needles and perhaps act out yourself with your best student. Your object is to ask for things in a shop and practise structures like 'have got', 'any', 'don't want'. The improvisation might start like this:

C: (*Coughs*) Good morning.
S.A.: (*Knitting*) What?
C: Good morning.
S.A.: Oh – Good morning.
C: (*Reaches out a trembling hand*) Twenty Gauloises please!
S.A.: Twenty what?
C: (*Impatiently*) Twenty Gauloises.
S.A.: What are they?
C: French cigarettes of course!
S.A.: French cigarettes. We haven't got any. (*Continues knitting*)
C: (*More impatiently. Coughs*) You haven't got any! Why not!
S.A.: We've only got English cigarettes!
C: I don't like English cigarettes!
And so on –

Notice, here, that the situation is simple. The greater the characterisation, the more students involve themselves, and the more variations will they produce. However, if the situation doesn't catch fire, don't work it to death. The aim is to produce something spontaneously and it's better to practise briefly than to fill a longer period with uninspired pauses.

You may find it easier to mix more automatic reactions with spontaneity. For instance, you have two people going into a restaurant. The 'waiter' greets them. The table is only laid with one fork and one spoon. The 'customers' ask for glasses, knives and another fork and spoon. You have given these to the other students in the class, so the 'waiter' has to ask them for the cutlery. Then the 'customers' order. They ask for all sorts of things, but the restaurant has only got one dish in each course left, so they have to order this. In this way, you practise 'Can we have ....' 'Have you got ....' 'We haven't got any ... left.' The 'customers' express impatience and the 'waiter' is indifferent, or apologetic.

When the 'customers' have ordered, the 'waiter' goes off, and you then switch to complete improvisation. They are an engaged couple, or a couple of business men, or two people who haven't seen each other for a long time, and they improvise accordingly. They go on as long as you want, and then, after calling in vain for the waiter at the top of their voices, they depart for another, better restaurant.

As this development has various stages, you get different groups of students to take part in turn. Three students act out the stage of asking for cutlery. Another group goes through it again. Another group repeats, and goes on to the ordinary stage. Yet another group goes through the first two stages, and then improvises conversation. Finally, another group goes through the whole thing including the departure.

Through the device of getting the waiter to ask students for cutlery, you also involve others in the class.

You also vary character and mood. You make the waiter now obsequious, now flippant, now surly. You make the couple in love, or impatient, or confused. You bring in 'props': cutlery, a menu, a cloth to put over the waiter's arm.

With more advanced classes, you can give fuller reign to role playing. You can introduce it by playing a tape or showing a film and then getting the students to produce their own versions of the situation. One course in commercial English,[1] has a series of films unfolding character and story in a factory. You show one of the films and the students adopt character roles and improvise in a similar situation. I have used dialogues from *Choosing your English*,[2] representing a couple disturbed late at night by an unknown visitor who says he knows a friend of theirs and wants a bed, or an angry couple going into an estate agent who has sold them the wrong house, or a couple hitch-hiking who find the driver is drunk and have to persuade him to stop the car and let them out. Once the class is familiar with the basic dialogue, they improvise according to the characters you have given them.

Another way is to get your students to perform a definite sketch, and then to produce variations. With large classes, you could act out a political meeting with hecklers. Then you split the class up into groups and they devise different themes for the public meeting: Pollution, Republicanism, etc. You have an agent introducing the speaker, the speaker himself: and perhaps the speaker's wife or husband appeals for quiet whenever necessary. The rest of the class take on the role of spontaneous hecklers.

In improvisation of this sort, you need a 'guillotine'. Thus, you might have a clock on the table. 'What's that ticking noise?' asks the speaker's wife or husband. 'It's a bomb,' shouts a heckler in the 'audience', and everyone gets up

---

1 *The Bellcrest File*, O.U.P., 1972.
2 Haycraft, J., *Choosing your English*, BBC Publications, 1972.

in panic and runs off. With this device you can end the improvisation whenever you want.

The important thing, then, is to provide a framework which encourages improvisation by way of a situation, a taped dialogue, a film or a sketch. At more elementary levels, it is important to link this with structure, idiom or certain areas of Social English which you want to practise. At more advanced stages, you can give more freedom to your students. It is essential, too, not to feel that you *have* to produce something sophisticated or 'brilliant' – it is the students who do most of the acting. The starting point is often something which seems naive but which, when transformed by the students' imaginations, can be amusing, and a good rehearsal for English outside the classroom.

These, then, are some suggestions for oral practice in the classroom. For other activities, see Chapters 10 and 11 on audio-visual aids – flashcards, wallcharts, and pictures for oral composition.

Further reading

1   Byrne, D., *Teaching Oral English*, Longman, 1986.

2   Rivers, Wilga, *Teaching Foreign Language Skills*, University of Chicago Press, 1980.

3   Littlewood, W., *Communicative Language Teaching*, CUP, 1983.

4   Revel, J., *Teaching Techniques for Communicative English*, Macmillan, 1979.

5   Holden, S., *Visual Aids for Classroom Interaction*, MEP.

Discussion

1   In what ways can acting out, improvisation and role playing help language learning?

2   What points would you have to keep in mind to ensure that conversation is a useful activity for everyone in the class? How can you make sure that everyone participates? To what extent would you deviate from your lesson plan to allow spontaneous conversation to develop?

3   Why is story-telling a useful language activity?

Exercises

1   Think up an initial situation which could be a starting point for improvisation at intermediate level.

Describe the characters, attitudes and mannerisms for this situation. What props would you use?

What language items would you be practising?

2   Make up a mime story designed to practise irregular verbs with an intermediate group. Describe the stages for using this in class.

9 Other language activities

9.1. Games

Games are an agreeable way of getting a class to use its initiative in English. As they are gently competitive, they increase motivation. They are also a contrast to periods of intensive study.

The competitive principle can be used for almost any form of revision. With irregular verbs, put up the names of your students and give them a mark for each verb they get right in context. If you want to practise question forms at elementary levels, get one student to think of an object in the classroom or wall chart, while the others guess what it is: 'Is it the door?' 'Is it Maria's chair?' etc. If you are practising nationalities, get one student to think of a famous painter or public figure, and the class guess his nationality and then his name: 'Are you English?' 'Are you Dutch?', etc.

When you are planning a lesson, ask yourself how you can bring in the games element. It is not difficult to devise games, yourself. Here is a game created by two teacher trainees, after two weeks on a course. They wanted to consolidate the contrasts: 'He works in the country' – 'He *doesn't* work in the country'. One of the trainees thought of a profession and the class had to suggest an activity which the profession might or might not perform. If the guess was correct, it was written down under the positive heading; if not, under the negative. If the students didn't guess the profession before ten sentences had been put up, they 'lost'.

The profession chosen was 'a country postman' and by the time the class had guessed it, the columns on the board were as follows:

Negative		Positive	
He doesn't	work in an office live in a town. drive a car. wear a suit.	He	travels. wears a uniform. rides a bicycle. lives in the country.

When guessing, students asked a question beginning with 'Does ...?' The teacher shook his head or nodded, and pointed to another student who then produced the answer. Another student then wrote it on the board. Thus, the teacher's role was simply to correct pronunciation or structure.

e.g.
Student 1: Does he live in a town?
Teacher: (shakes his head).

Student 2: He doesn't live in a town.

Student 3: (writes the statement in the left hand column)

Games should lend themselves to certain teaching aims. Thus, 'Alibi' is useful for question and answer in the past. Create a crime situation and divide your class into pairs, who each devise an alibi: 'Where were you at the time of the crime?', 'When did you arrive there?', 'When did you leave?', 'What was the place like?', 'What were you wearing?', 'What were you doing?', etc. When everyone is ready, one of the pair goes outside and the other is quizzed. The other then comes in and is quizzed in turn. If the answers agree, then the alibi is established. If they don't, the couple are guilty.

There are a number of books available describing more games you can play in the classroom (see end of chapter – also word games: 5.2.13.). When going through them, try to imagine applying these games to the particular students you have. Be careful, though, not to go on too long and remember that most party games are unknown outside Anglo Saxon countries. ✕

9.2. Songs

These are another useful change of activity and are particularly useful when structured with vocabulary chosen for a certain level. You can then use them for consolidation and practice. They are a welcome contrast after a hard comprehension passage or drilling, and they are good for bringing the class together. Teach them in a lively way.

Here are some variations, using songs recorded on tape:

(a) Play the tape as many times as necessary and ask questions.

(b) Get the class to sing line by line, following the tape.

(c) Show students the script and get the class to sing it through, following the tape. Clear up queries on vocabulary or idiom.

(d) Divide up the class and have a group, each singing a line or verse. Re-play the tape as often as necessary. Find out who has a good voice, and try to get solos. Bring out a student to conduct. Try different combinations until the song is familiar.

(e) Play and sing whenever you want to revise. It's a good idea to play songs at the beginning of a class, while everyone is settling down.

Pop or traditional songs can also be useful. The problem, though is often vocabulary. 'What shall we do with the drunken sailor?' is fine for practising questions in the future, adjectives before nouns and intonation patterns. However, with 'early' pronounced 'earligh', and words like 'hoist' and 'scuppers' you have to consider whether you are likely to spend more time on uncommon vocabulary than the teaching value warrants.

Try to have folk evenings as part of club activities. Then you can teach indirectly through pop or traditional songs, concentrating on enjoyment, without needing to explain everything.

In the classroom, make sure that you use songs with the teaching objectives firmly in mind. However, also try to catch the mood of the class: use songs when students are tired, or need cheering up, or when you are near the end of term. You may then be able to teach as much without their realising it, as when you press them to learn.

9.3. Projects

Here, students can try to solve problems outside the classroom. These can range from simple tasks such as looking for something in a local English paper, to making radio programmes in English, or using local libraries for research into English or American writers, politicians, etc.

With individual projects, there is the advantage of variety, as each student explores a particular area which is then disseminated to the rest of the class. Here are a few examples of projects:

In a non-English speaking country, get each student or group:

(a) to 'adopt' an English town and find out everything possible about it;

(b) to make a study of the equivalent industry or trade they or their fathers work in, in some English speaking country;

(c) to meet one English, American, or Commonwealth person and discover as much about him/her as possible;

(d) to discover what any one other person outside the school thinks of some aspect of Britain or America or the Commonwealth – whether fashion, pop, literature, national character or some recent political development.

In an English speaking country, get each student or group:

(a) to go to a pub, market, shop, etc. and note down any conversation he had, or overheard:

(b) to go to any interesting place and describe it, illustrating this perhaps with photographs;

(c) to research and record a day in the life of any particular professional person: policeman, solicitor, pub owner, etc.:

(d) to observe people in any crowded place, whether bus, tube, park, etc., and comment on the differences in dress, behaviour and so on from a similar group in his own country.

Projects such as these also encourage the student to speak to people, or to go to places which might be interesting. Because he has a particular aim, the student will involve himself more with life around him.

Think up projects which suit individual students and the place you are teaching in. Be careful not to 'commit a nuisance' by, for instance, sending all your students to one flustered travel agent in order to find out details of a journey they have no intention of making.

9.4. Homework

The classroom should be the generator from which spring all sorts of other activities in English. It is, therefore, essential to encourage your students to do homework and to 'reward' them for doing it. Don't give them so much that they feel overburdened by it – nor so little that you fail to use their potential to the full. Homework is also a valuable way of getting to know your class better: as you correct, you become aware of individual strengths and weaknesses.

Give your students homework that interests them, with as much variety as possible. Ask yourself what particular secondary skills (p. 18) they should be practising. Also make demands on their powers of deduction, narration, description, etc. You are more likely to get homework done if you set written work which has to be handed in. If you set something that has to be learnt or read, check that it has been done, even if you are teaching adults.

Some techniques encourage students to do homework. Thus, don't collect it all together, but ask for it individually, so that those who have not done it will have to say so in front of everyone else. Again, give it back individually for the same reason. You can do this with adults too, so long as you are not officious, but are simply creating a situation where they have to make excuses.

Mark your register with homework results as well as attendance. A student may be lagging behind because he hasn't done homework for some time – a fact of which you could be unaware of if you haven't marked it down.

Your students should have two workbooks: one they hand in and one for current use. Ensure that these are kept up carefully, so that they are both a source of revision and a record of progress. Perusade your students to write on every other line, so that you can correct clearly.

Some classroom time will have to be devoted to preparing and going over homework.

Further reading

1 Wilson, K., *Mr Monday and other songs for the teaching of English*, Longman, 1971.

2 Wilson, K., *Goodbye Rainbow*, Longman, 1974.

3 Kingsbury, R. H., and O'Shea, P., *Sunday Afternoons*, Longman, 1973.

4 Abbs, B., and York, N., *Skyhigh*, Longman, 1975.

5 Wright, A., *Games for Language Learning*, CUP, 1984.

6 Revell, J., *Teaching Techniques for Communicative English*, Macmillan, 1979.

Discussion

1 What are the advantages and disadvantages of using games in the classroom?

2 Why is homework important?

Exercises

1   Either think up a game to practise 'some' and 'any', or describe how 'Twenty Questions' might be used in the classroom and what language items you would be practising.

2   You have 15 minutes to teach a song with the tape recorder. The song is at the right level for your class and there are only 3 words in it they don't know. Describe how you would use the 15 minutes.

3   Outline some useful projects you could set for students studying English in their own countries.

10 Audio-visual aids

Much of what we say in any language is prompted by what we see or have seen around us. We, therefore, have to give our students practice in reacting in English to objects, or pictures. Apart from this, aids are an addition to our 'armoury'. They allow us to explain a word or concept simply, by showing a picture, or pointing to an object. Abstractions can often be expressed in this way where mime or words are insufficient. Again, the manoeuvrability of objects or pictures is a great advantage. Time can be saved by passing pictures or objects round the class and getting group work going; revision can derive from the re-introduction of visual aids; tempo can be accelerated because showing or pointing is a more rapid process than speaking or explaining.

Naturally, you choose aids for specific purposes. Objects can be more evocative than pictures, e.g. real money, tickets, cheques, etc. On the other hand, some pictures can be more evocative than objects and easier to handle, e.g. food displays, ocean liners, fashion pictures, etc. Wall charts bring more ideas, or things, together than simple pictures, and are useful for extensive descriptions and provoking dialogues, situations and stories.

Don't however, become intoxicated with visual aids. Once they have been produced, there is sometimes a regrettable tendency to use them for everything. They can deteriorate into poor substitutes for preparing a lesson. Combine them with other teaching techniques to fulfil immediate and long term aims. In the end, it comes down to a simple question of budgets. Is it better to buy and maintain projectors, or to have better blackboards, or more English magazines, or more expensive and varied textbooks, or more comfortable classrooms? The answer can only come from the person on the spot who knows his or her students.

In any case, be careful not to turn mechanical aids into gimmicks. It's easy to forget that your students learn mainly through the actual quality of your teaching and *how* you use your materials, whether you are using turbine driven, multi-technicolour projectors, or sand on a beach to sketch out illustrations for a class in the open.

10.1. Objects

Reference has already been made to using *classroom objects* for presenting vocabulary and structure. The great advantage is that everything is at hand and familiar to the students. However, refrain from excessive use of 'blackboard',

99

'pencils', 'rubber', and other objects which are not commonly used outside the classroom.

The structural practice you can extract is almost limitless: prepositions – putting objects 'on' or 'in' or 'near' other objects; placing something in a corner, or on the table, or under a chair and practising 'It's been there for ...'; comparatives – so many things are bigger, smaller, lower, or higher than other ones; where things were yesterday, or where they may be tomorrow; things people have, or haven't got, in pockets, in their wallets, hands, and so on.

The scope is increased by *bringing in objects*. It always helps to set a scene with 'props'. If you're practising a dialogue in a restaurant, try to bring in the cutlery. Telephone conversations are enhanced by bringing in toy telephones and getting students to sit back to back so they can't see one another. If you've got a policeman in a dialogue, give him a toy helmet. This will not only intrigue and thus involve your students, but also set the tone for acting out. It is also important to take advantage of particular objects at hand in the country where you are teaching. For example, in Japan it is easy to get hold of books of matches with the names of different hotels and night clubs on them, and in one class I saw the teacher was practising 'was/were' by giving a book of matches to each student. Question and answer practice went as follows:

'Were you at the Hotel San Bancho last night?'
'No, I was at the Jimbo-Cho coffee bar.'

and so on.

Ideally, all classes of technical English should have access to machinery or models. Teaching everyday terms for aeroplanes or cars is likely to be more effective with models than with charts or drawings. Alternatively, make your classroom into the appropriate environment: the best place to teach immigrant factory workers is probably in the factory itself.

Precise *descriptions of objects* in the classroom can also be useful. For advanced classes, emphasise that you want the description to include size, shape, surface, colour, function and aesthetic appeal – if any. Then even describing an ashtray becomes a difficult exercise in precision and vocabulary:

'It's made of glass – it's about six inches in diameter and three inches high. It's bluish. It's square, with the sides sloping down from the outer edges for about an inch, and then dropping perpendicularly for about another inch down to the tray itself. It's got a smooth surface. It's used for stubbing out cigarettes and dropping ash. It's a very commonplace ashtray which I wouldn't particularly like to have at home, but it's useful because it's fairly big and would take a lot of cigarettes.'

You would, of course, tailor the description to the level of the class.

10.2. People

Often forgotten is the practice which *the students* themselves can provide physically, not to mention *the teacher* and his capacity for mime, demonstration, and so on. Thus a good exercise for practising stress with the letter 'h' using all the students is: HER hair's brown and HIS hair's BLACK and HER hair's FAIR and HIS hair's DARK etc. The verbs 'have got' or 'wear' or 'has got on' are obvious ones for use with the students themselves.

Valuable also is the use of the students' experience. The first thing people normally have to do in a foreign language is to ask and answer personal questions: 'What's your name?' 'Where are you from?' 'What do you do?' etc. They also need to identify themselves:

'I'm Roberto. I'm Italian. I'm from Milan. I'm a student.' etc.

Teaching through identification brings the class together, as they get to know more about one another – particularly if nationalities are mixed. It can bring its own problems: with adults you get complicated professions like 'interior decorator' or 'computer engineer'. However, students do need to state their own professions early on and it is therefore worth overcoming these difficulties at the beginning.

Identification of this kind is of value also for revision. As you progress, each student can give a summary of him/herself which grows more and more complete. You then get another student to repeat what has been said, thus practising the ability to understand, remember and reproduce, and to get him talking about another person in English. At more advanced levels, you can draw on personal experience more and more – a film that one of them has seen, their homes, experiences of childhood, or any other reminiscences students want to express. This also helps you to get to know your students better and thus enables you to gear your teaching to what interests them.

10.3. The blackboard

This is one of the most important visual aids, commonly available and inexpensive. It has the advantage of providing a focal point of attention for the whole class, and can be used for a variety of purposes. However, it is very easy to forget its usefulness, simply because it is always there, or to use it ineffectively through lack of thought, preparation, and reluctance to regard it as an integral part of a lesson.

When using the blackboard, certain points should be borne in mind:

Prepare your blackboard work in advance and ask yourself before the lesson how you can use it best to fulfil your particular teaching aims. Start with a clean board. Write/draw clearly – so that all the pupils can see, even those at the back of the class. Use the left hand side for current work and the right for keeping a record of the work done during the lesson. Correct spelling and punctuation are obviously essential. Practise a good, clear, legible hand, and learn to draw simply and unambiguously on the board.

Be careful that you don't stand for a long time writing on the board with your back to the class while students do nothing, and don't talk to the board – if you need to say something, turn round and address the class. Keep the students involved by getting them to read and repeat parts of what you have written. You can also get them to write on the board for you, and test their spelling this way.

Clean the board when it becomes impossibly crowded, instead of squeezing in additional sentences wherever there is space. If your students have a clear visual image of what you have written, this will help them. If everything is mixed up, you are merely using the board to confuse them.

10.4. Flash cards

These are cards on which words and/or pictures are printed or drawn. They should be big enough to be seen clearly by every student in the class. There are published sets of flash cards on the market, but they are also easy to make either as drawings, or with cut out pictures from magazines. Durability can be increased by proper mounting. Use cardboard and cover them with transpaseal so that they don't get smudged.

Flash cards can be used for consolidating vocabulary, practising structure and word order, or for a variety of games. They are simple and effective, but they also require careful thought and preparation in advance.

10.4.1. Word cards

When practising word order, have a number of cards representing all the words in a sentence. For example, if you are practising asking questions in the past, you can have the following word cards:

| DOCTOR | SAY | ITALIAN | DID | THE | ? | WHAT |

The cards can be fixed to the board, or given to a student, and arranged correctly either by the class as a whole or individual students, to form:

| WHAT | DID | THE | ITALIAN | DOCTOR | SAY | ? |

The same technique could be used to practise structure. You want to consolidate 'was/were'. You jumble up two possible sentences:

| . | . | TIRED | WERE | AT | THEY | SCHOOL | WAS | HE |

These are sorted out to form:

| HE | WAS | TIRED | . | THEY | WERE | AT | SCHOOL | . |

Here, the students, as well as getting the correct word order have to make a structure choice as well.

Similar exercises are effective if the class is divided into small groups. Each student is given a number of cards and puts down what he regards as the most likely word to start a sentence, for example, THEY. The next student puts down ARE, and they continue until a finished sentence is formed.

Another way is to give each group the same word cards. In a given time, each tries to form the maximum number of sentences, which are then read out to the rest of the class. The competitive element here can make it interesting and lively.

Games with word cards are also effective. For example, you can practise the First Conditional with sets of cards, perhaps representing different kinds of meat, vegetables, dairy products and so on. Each student puts down a card and tries to exchange it in order to get a complete set:

'If you give me some carrots, I'll give you some butter.'

and so on.

The game can also be played with money cards:

'If you give me 50p I'll give you some potatoes.'

and so on.

Another game that can be played in small groups is to have each student taking a card in turn from a pile, until he can form a sentence. Whoever forms most sentences wins.

Word cards can also be used with complete sentences. For example, one student holds up a card 'Are you learning French?'. The others have to find appropriate answers, e.g. 'No.' 'We're learning English' and so on.

10.4.2. Picture cards

These are useful for presenting, practising and revising vocabulary or as prompts for other activities – for example, to illustrate the characters in a dialogue, to help students improvise. They can be used as prompts for simple substitution drills. Instead of saying a word, you hold up a card. For example, to practise the following:

$$
\left.\begin{array}{l} \text{He's} \\ \text{She's} \\ \text{They've} \end{array}\right\} \text{got} \quad \begin{array}{l} \text{a} \\ \\ \text{an} \end{array} \left\{\begin{array}{l} \text{car.} \\ \text{bicycle.} \\ \text{aeroplane.} \end{array}\right.
$$

Here, you could have two sets of cards – one showing he, she, they, and the other showing the objects, which is more flexible than one set of cards showing the whole sentence.

 He

 Car

 She

 Bicycle

 They

 Aeroplane

Picture cards are also useful for identifying verbs of action. You can introduce the verbs with mime one day and revise them with picture cards the next. For example:

He's climbing a mountain.
She's going downstairs.

Cards can be used to revise or introduce prepositions: 'He's diving into the swimming pool', etc., or for verb tenses – 'He's going to dive into the swimming pool'.

The same cards can be used for practising different points, so once you have made cards, you can build up a library.

Cards can also be used to indicate a sequence. 'He offered her a cigarette'. 'He lit it.' You can link more cards together to get a sequence long enough to elaborate a short story, practising a variety of points and getting the class to help build up the story together, ask and answer questions, and so on. For example:

Show card:
    What was he doing?
    Was he alone?
    Who was he?

What happened?
Who opened the door?
Was it a ghost?
What do you think happened next?

Build up the story like this and then get them to revise by telling the complete story: 'One day, John was sitting alone reading, when suddenly the door opened …'

You can also choose cards which bring out specialised language: give out pictures of people, known or famous. Get the students to describe features and expressions and say what they think of the individual's character, and perhaps imagine other things about their life, and so on. If you use pictures of famous people, you can then tell them what the person was really like. As you have already made the class think about the portrait, they will be more interested in the original and will want to know if their estimation of character was accurate.

Pictures can also be used with pronunciation teaching, by having cards depicting different sounds – for example 'heart'; 'hat'; 'hut'; 'sleep'; 'slip'; etc., or verbs of action ending with similar sounds in the past:

'id': counted, added, roasted, etc.
'ed': smiled, climbed, opened, closed, etc.
't': asked, worked, typed, laughed, etc.

or variations in the third person singular:

's' – counts, roasts, asks
'iz' – pushes, dances, touches
'z' – smiles, climbs, opens.

Cards can also be used to practise stress shift, for example:

A dog

A BIG dog,

a SMALL dog,

a CAT

a WHITE cat

a BLACK cat

a black DOG and so on.

10.4.3. Combining word and picture cards

Show a word card and the student(s) must find the right picture card, or vice versa. Or divide the class into two teams. A student on one side flashes a picture card and a student on the other finds the appropriate word card, or vice versa.

10.5. Wall charts

In the first part of this book, we examined wall charts used for introducing new vocabulary. We linked it with structure practice and straightforward descriptions.

Wall charts are particularly valuable for practising the Present Continuous, but also prepositions, question words, 'going to', 'has just', and the Past – as long as you establish this clearly enough by writing YESTERDAY, or LAST MONTH, on top of the board. A good place for a wall chart is next to the blackboard, or on the board itself, so that you can write up relevant words next to it. Ensure that the picture is big enough for everyone to see details.

Wall charts are also useful for drills. You simply point at the prompts instead of saying them. For intance, you are using a chart of a shopping scene. Your model sentence is 'He wants to buy some cheese'.

Visual Prompts

Butter	He wants to buy some butter.
A woman customer and cheese.	She wants to buy some cheese.
Two customers and oranges.	They want to buy some oranges.
etc.	etc.

This process is easier if you use a baton to indicate parts of the chart.

You can also use charts to elaborate dialogues (in social situations). A picture of a railway station allows you to focus on a lady at the newsagent's:

'Daily Mail, please.'
'Sorry. There aren't any left.'

'Daily Express, then.'

'Twelve p. please.'

'Thank you.'

Dialogues obviously depend on what you are trying to do, and on the English your students know. Vary them by introducing personalities, e.g. the woman is grumpy and the newsagent polite (see p. 88).

As with flash cards, you can use wall charts for discussing personalities, particularly at more advanced levels when most of the vocabulary is known. You have a picture of a family at home in the evening. What do your students think the father is like? The mother? The children? How can personalities be judged by their expressions, by what they are wearing, by what they are doing?

Using the wall chart in this way, you can also examine the social background in English or American terms. What are the children's schools like? Is the father a member of a trade union? If the mother works, what sort of job could she do? Prepare your own ideas first, so that you can prompt with suggestions if few are forthcoming. If a lot of suggestions are made, choose the most sensible, and build up from there, so that at the end there is an established picture of the family, which you can then get your class to describe for homework.

From this, get your students to construct a story. Has there been a quarrel or some disastrous news? Are they waiting for something, or has something occurred of which, as yet, they know nothing? Will the telephone ring or will there be a caller? Again, it's best to prepare a story yourself. Although it's important that your students create the story, you will probably only get the tempo you need if you prompt them.

Ideally, you should build up a wall chart as a continual form of revision. If you have practised vocabulary or structure with it, go over this before you embark on something new. Be careful, though, that your students don't get bored with the same picture. Use a number of wall charts alternatively for snap revision or consolidation. If you do this successfully, your students will be reminded of words and structure which they have previously learnt, each time you put one up. If you bring out personality, situation and imaginative incident, your students will also recall these when you use the wall chart again.

A wall chart, then, when properly used, has all the advantages of a visual summary which can be apprehended immediately. Use some practical way of hanging it up, such as Blu-tak or Plasti-tak.

10.6. Pictures for oral composition

This usually refers to a number of pictures which make up a story. Have them either as wall pictures, stencilled so each student has a copy, or on an overhead projector transparency. As with other visual aids, students can describe each picture, separately. Once this is done, however, you can get your students to go from description to story telling. Picture composition can also be developed into written summaries on the board and used to practise narrative skills in homework.

Let us go briefly through different phases of teaching picture composition at the intermediate level. These can be varied in many ways, and the following are only suggestions:

1 DESCRIPTION

Get your students to describe the pictures. Give relevant, new vocabulary where needed, or you can do this by way of question and answer, and then piece everything together.

2 QUESTION AND ANSWER

Ask yourself what question forms you want to practise, e.g. 'Is/Are?' 'Do/ Does?' 'Did?' 'How many?' 'What?' 'Who?' 'Why?' 'Which?'

Get the students to ask each other questions. Prompt if necessary by indicating the kind of questions, or tense, or question word you want:

First picture

1 *Is* Mr Flash a newsagent?
2 *Are* they selling shoes?
3 *Do* the children come to Flash Stores every day?
4 *Does* the owner smoke a pipe?

Second picture

5 *Did* they build a garage?
6 *How many* cars are parked outside Joy Stores?
7 *What* is Mr Flash doing on the pavement?
8 *Who* are looking reproachfully at their employer?
9 *Why* is everyone going to Joy Stores?
10 *Which* store has most customers?

3 STRUCTURE PRACTICE

Third Conditional, although you could choose others.

If Flash Stores hadn't raised/increased their prices ...

the other store wouldn't/be there/have been built/have opened.

they wouldn't have lost/their customers/money.

the owner would still be/happy/earning money/smoking a cigar/sitting at his cash desk.

the children would still/buy their sweets and ice cream there/come to the shop/ store.

4 DIALOGUES

Get your students to make up dialogues, acting them out. Set the situations: What did the customers say when the prices were raised? What did the owners of Joy Stores say to one another before deciding to build a new shop? What did they say to one another when their shop was so successful? What did Mr and Mrs Flash say to one another when Flash Stores was suddenly empty? What did the shop assistants in Flash Stores say to each other about their employers when the shop was empty?

Let's take the last one as an example. Here is one of many possibilities:

S.A. 1: If he hadn't raised the prices!
S.A. 2: There was no need. The rent must be the same. Certainly our salaries haven't gone up.

S.A. 1 : Now we'll lose our jobs.
S.A. 2 : Probably. And he'll go bankrupt.
S.A. 1 : Look he's crying!
S.A. 2 : Well, it's his own fault!

5   STORY TELLING

Work out the sequence of the narrative first yourself. Then elicit a few sentences from each of your students in turn.

'Well, there was a shop called Flash Stores, which sold sweets, chocolates and ice cream. As there was a school nearby, the shop was always crowded with schoolchildren when school was finished. The owner, though, was very greedy. He sat behind his cash desk and smoked a big cigar and thought about all the money he was earning. One day, he decided to raise the prices. He put a notice in the shop window saying that there was an increase in prices owing to rising costs. . . .' etc.

6   SUMMARISING

Get your students to summarise the *essential* elements. Pay special attention to pronunciation and the dramatic element.

'There was a shop called Flash Stores near a school, and all the children went there to buy sweets, chocolates and ice cream. The owner was very greedy and one day he raised all the prices. However, on the other side of the road, another shop was being built. When it opened, it charged lower prices and all the customers went there instead of to Flash Stores. The greedy owner stood on the pavement and wept as he looked at the queues of customers outside his rival's shop.'

Write up the sentences while the students are summarising, or get the students to write them down.

7   DISCUSSION

What do you think the owner of Flash Stores will do now? Can any of you remember anything similar happening in your own home town? Should Mr Flash have raised his prices? Do you think shops should be allowed to compete like this or should the State own them? etc.

8   HOMEWORK

Get the students to answer specific questions, or to write a summary of the story of the characters.

9   REVISION

Return to the pictures some time later making sure that anything new is consolidated.

You can, of course, practise all this in many different ways. You could, for instance, do the first picture on one day, and the second later – which would enable you to revise most of the vocabulary before getting on to the second picture. You could tape your version of the story and play it *before* you show them the picture composition, which you could then use for direct narrative.

You could also use the picture composition with only one specific object in mind, e.g. structure, or increasing vocabulary, or getting the students to work out the story on paper, themselves, without preparation. It depends on *why* they are using the picture composition and on how much variety you need.

10.7. Overhead projector transparencies

You write or draw on a transparency, and project it onto a screen. The transparencies can easily be added to, while the lesson is in progress. The O.P. is a useful alternative to the blackboard in that the teacher doesn't have to turn his back on the students, and he can save time by preparing the material in advance. Another advantage over the blackboard is that the O.P. does not have to be cleaned and there is more space available. It is used in much the same way as the blackboard – for writing model sentences, presentation, explanation, drills, pictures, etc. Some commercially produced transparencies are also available and it's also possible, with the aid of a special machine, to copy pictures onto them.

Overhead projector transparencies can be flexibly used – it's possible to place several transparencies over each other to build up more detail gradually, or the teacher can mask out parts of the picture with a piece of paper to focus and direct students' attention.

10.8. Slides and film strips

Film strips are similar to slides except that they are easier to use, as all the pictures come on a roll, and you can switch from one to another without worrying whether the pictures are upside down or in the wrong order. Otherwise, both slides and film strips have the same function as wall charts, flash cards, or pictures for oral composition. The advantage is that you can move from one to the other more easily once the equipment is set up. You can make your own slides for any form of lecture. They are particularly useful for any series: for instance, a routine day in someone's life, or talking about London or New York, or for some specialist subject such as the manufacture of plastics, or the oil industry.

10.9. Film

Obviously, this accustoms students to understanding English in the cinema or on television. Usefulness can be increased by making sure of 'feed-back'.

1 Choose specialised films for different professions, e.g. doctors, engineering, etc.

2 See the film before you show it so that you can determine level and suitability of content.

3 Stop the film from time to time, and get students to ask questions, if they have not understood. Then, ask them questions about events, character, description, etc. If you do this, you will find you can ease your students into

understanding the film more effectively, and that they retain more of what they hear and see.

4   Give the students a script of the film, after they have seen it. Get them to go over it for homework and ask them to write a summary, or to give you an oral account next day. You can of course do this with or without a script, but if you can get hold of one, it allows students to work more on their own, and to synchronise the spoken and written commentaries. Obviously, you can only do this with fairly short films.

However much you use films in class, also encourage your students to go to the cinema and watch television. If you can, give them a weekly list of coming films and television programmes which you think could benefit them.

Films can also be used more directly in class and a number have been produced specifically for language teaching. With special equipment, the teacher can start the film, stop it, go back and go forward and in this way, use the film in any way he wants, whether for presentation, practice or revision.

10.10.   Video

This is less expensive than people imagine. In fact, setting up a complete video unit costs less than a language laboratory. However, little material is as yet available. This has an advantage: it is necessary to produce one's own material, tailored to immediate needs. As video tape is no more expensive than sound tape, and as video is no more difficult to operate than a tape recorder, video can thus be used creatively as a very useful adjunct:

1   Use it for filming trainee teachers. It can teach them a lot about technique, their relations with students, their mannerisms, etc.
2   Co-operate with other teachers in acting out suitable sketches; show these on video as a model, before students act out, themselves. This is particularly valuable for 'Social English'.
3   Record films from T.V. programmes. This is useful for specialised study: an interview with a famous modern novelist; a Shakespeare play; a specialist film on new developments in medicine, etc. If the film is only used in your school and not sold, there should be little objection as far as copyright is concerned.
4   Film the students themselves as they act out dialogues. The fact that they can see themselves speaking English on film is stimulating and can encourage them. It also helps them get over the 'nervousness barrier'. if you can encourage them to speak boldly on film, they are more likely to do so when speaking English outside the classroom. As you can stop the video film when you want to, and go backwards and forwards, this is invaluable for vivid correction.

10.11.   Tape recorders

A tape recorder is an essential classroom aid. In the first place, it brings other voices into the classroom and gives the students valuable practice in listening to varieties of English different from the teacher's. A great deal of material is available on tape and you can also record your own from the radio, by getting other teachers to record material for you, taping conversations in shops, pubs, in the street, and so on. If the students have cassette recorders and you have the tapes, there is also scope for setting them homework, based on tape.

As with all mechanical aids, precision in use is essential. Without proficient control, hours can be wasted trying to find the place, erasing when you should be listening, and so on. Practise recording and playing back until you are proficient. Set the tape up at the appropriate place before the lesson begins. Ideally, use a tape recorder with a number gauge so that you can wind back to any part of the passage without losing the way.

Tape material can be effectively used for listening comprehension work (see Chapter 7) and it can also be used in connection with other activities – dialogues (8.1), songs (9.2.) and so on. You can also use the tape recorder to record students. Some students, particularly if they are advanced, think their spoken English is much better than it is. Get them to talk briefly about some simple subject such as a description of their home town, their school, the house or flat they live in, and so on. Then play it through, with the class commenting on the mistakes, and revise.

For every thirty seconds of recording you need about five minutes of correction, comment and organisation, unless your class is brilliant. As you probably cannot include everyone in a single lesson, spread recordings out: do one or two each lesson, or get two or more students talking to each other.

With more advanced students, you can get them to write and record broadcasts in English, or, if you are teaching in an English-speaking country, get them to go round interviewing and recording 'natives'.

10.12. The language laboratory

The language laboratory became a controversial issue immediately it was introduced. There were those who attacked it as a mechanical, soulless device which would eliminate the teacher, and as a commercial gimmick which 'conned' the students into thinking they were being taught in a modern, and therefore effective, way. On the other side, many supporters saw it as a solution to all teaching problems, and imagined that all you had to do was to enclose a student in a booth with a tape, whereupon, like a chrysalis turning into a butterfly, he would emerge transformed and speaking a new language perfectly.

Taking a moderate view, the language laboratory is a useful teaching aid, just as the blackboard and flash cards are. Like a car, it has to be properly serviced and maintained. It requires someone on the spot who can untwist a tape or clean a recording head without having to call a mechanic. It also needs a considerable store of tapes which wear out and have to be replaced. A language laboratory is, therefore, both expensive to buy and costly to run effectively. It has to take the space of a classroom unless a portable laboratory is used.

There are several kinds of laboratory:

10.12.1. Listening laboratory

In this type of lab, each student has a tape recorder with a head set and simply listens to a tape, going back as often as he wishes. He is, therefore, able to work at his own speed.

This is the cheapest form of laboratory. It concentrates on the single skill of listening and understanding which, in the classroom, is often underplayed. It is useful for specialised English as each student can listen to different passages.

There are several ways of using this laboratory:

Get the student to listen without a text and work out the meaning by himself.

Get the student to listen without a text and allow him to use a dictionary. The disadvantage is that time will be spent searching for words whose spelling is uncertain.

Get the student to listen while he follows the text on paper, thus linking the spoken and written word.

Append oral questions at the end of the passage and the student has to work through until he feels he can answer the questions satisfactorily.

Test the student's memory by getting him to listen, and then take him back to the classroom to answer written questions on what he has just heard, or get him to take notes and prepare a written summary, or dictation.

Success depends on the quality and variety of the texts provided, and it is, therefore, necessary to build up a really good tape library.

Although this is the cheapest form of laboratory, it does provide practice in an essential skill. It does allow the student to work on his own, and it does make individual specialisation possible. It is also easier for the student to operate the machine, and monitoring is unnecessary. It fulfils the same kind of role as an exam or homework, with the student either working by himself in class time, or, after the class is over, on the written version.

10.12.2. Audio Active Laboratory (A.A.)

With this kind of laboratory there is a teacher's console and individual headsets. A tape is played from the console. The student listens and, when he speaks, he can hear his own voice through the headset. However, he cannot record. Everyone has to go at the speed of the tape being played. The teacher can listen to students and speak to them. However, while he is speaking to students, the tape is cut off.

The student does have an idea of whether his answer was right or wrong, and next time round he can try and produce a better version.

The effect is similar to a chorus drill where the student can hear his own voice more clearly, and the teacher can listen to individuals.

A laboratory like this is cheaper and easier to maintain than the A.A.C. Outside distractions are cut out by the headset, and it does provide variety as another form of practice.

However, much of what it achieves can be done in the classroom with a tape recorder and chorus drilling. The advantage of the student working at his own speed and correcting himself is lost. As a result, the student's personal sense of achievement is also less.

10.12.3. The Audio-Active-Comperative (A.A.C.)

This is the most complex and expensive type of laboratory. It consists of a console which allows the teacher to listen or speak to each student in turn, or alternatively to speak to all of them together. Through the console, the teacher can also record on all the students' tapes.

Each student is in a booth with a separate tape recorder and ear-phones. He controls the tape recorder by pushing a button or switching a lever, to 'Speak' – 'Listen' – 'Wind forward' – 'Rewind'. This means that he can record, or listen to what is already on the tape, or listen to what he has just said. He also has a button which he presses if he wants to communicate with the teacher.

This kind of laboratory has great advantages as a teaching aid. It allows the student the intensity of a private class, as he works on his own, progresses at his own speed and uses more of the time available for speaking than he would in a collective class. It is also good for the shyer student who expresses himself more confidently in his booth than in front of his class.

However, it is important to realise that the laboratory is not effective for presenting or teaching something new. Its merit lies in providing individual, intensive practice of what has already been understood. Because the teacher in charge cannot listen to everyone at once, students are encouraged to correct themselves, which is probably a more effective way of making the learner aware of new language than correction from outside.

The laboratory is particularly useful for consolidating structure, for accelerating rapid reactions to language prompts and for improving speech and fluency in forming sentences. It is useful for pronunciation, although some students have difficulty in recognising their own mistakes and need a lot of help before they can correct them. It is also useful for increasing the comprehension of short sentences. However, given that language laboratory time in any school is limited and expensive, it is advisable not to do anything in the lab that you can do in the classroom. Thus, it is probably best not to use note-taking or dictation passages so that you do not waste the recording facilities which are one of the principle advantages of an A.A.C. laboratory.

Many laboratory exercises are in the form of structural drills, which can be two-phase (prompt–response), three-phase (prompt–response–correct answer) or four-phase (prompt–response–correct answer–space for student to repeat the correct answer). The following is an example of a three-phase drill:

'Listen: I was in Rome.' (pause) 'When were you there?'
'Now you ask the questions:'

Prompt	Student response	Correct answer
I was in Rome	When were you there?	When were you there?
She was in Paris.	When was she there?	When was she there?
They were in New York.	When were they there?	When were they there?
He was in London.	When was he there?	When was he there?
We were in Tokyo.	When was you there?	When were you there?

Each exercise should be short with no more than five or six sentences, as the student should go over it again and again until it is right. The initial prompt should produce only one answer. Thus if your prompt were 'How are you?' the answer on the tape could be 'Fine, thank you' or 'Very well, thank you', or 'O.K., and you?' or 'Terrible' and so on. As only one of these alternatives can appear on the tape, the student could think his answer was wrong, simply because it did not correspond with the one given.

As a rule, it is better to train your students to listen to the prompts rather than to read them in their book. The value of the lab is the oral/aural practice it gives, and the sooner the students get used to responding to what is said to them the better. Likewise, it is absurd to have tapes which are unnaturally slow, or which do not use contractions, as students are then listening to and practising unnatural English.

There are, of course, other forms of laboratory drills than the one described above. Many of the oral drills described in 4.3. can be used, and the exercises can also be linked to pictures.

10.12.4. Classroom preparation

If the object of the laboratory is to make students more fully aware of new language and to get them to produce and practise it correctly, you need preparation beforehand in class, so that they can start work straightaway, clear in their own minds about what they have to do.

The best way is to play a tape of the laboratory exercises. Make sure that your class understand the instructions and that they become familiar with vocabulary, structure, idiom, and the intonation patterns. Then their laboratory work will really consist of consolidation, and they should be able to *use* orally what they have previously *understood* mentally.

Language laboratory work should also be an integral part of classroom planning and not something separate which is added on to classroom work.

The advantage of the laboratory is that it can do certain things better than you can. For one thing, its exercises are pre-planned precisely. For another, practise is more concentrated. You have, therefore, to introduce your students to what they are going to do in the laboratory, but at the same time do less in class because you are fortunate enough to have an additional aid which will do it for you, if you delegate properly.

10.12.5. Monitoring

Efficient monitoring is perhaps the most important part of language laboratory work and requires a lot of care and effort on the part of the teacher.

So as to include everyone, you have to follow a certain routine: monitor each student in numerical order at the beginning and make sure that they have all started work satisfactorily. Go back to them in this order, a second time. Then take the worst problems and try to deal with them. However, don't spend too much time on these as yet, unless you are sure everyone else is doing the exercises correctly. Later, when you and your students have got into it, you will know who finds it most difficult, and you can spend more time on them. Even later, concentrate on pronunciation as this is where students have most difficulty in correcting themselves.

A short cut is to have a tape in the students' language which explains all the mechanical instructions and can be played at the beginning. However, with or without the tape, an average class needs about three sessions to learn to work really smoothly.

When monitoring, make sure that students do one section of the exercise well, before they go on to the next. However, don't correct one student ad nauseam, or he/she will get jittery and therefore incapable. Correct briefly, and then come back later on. When you interrupt, only do so when the student is listening.

Find out, too, if the student has actually heard the mistake he has just made. If he hasn't, get him to re-wind and listen again. Only when he recognises his mistake and can tell you the correct version, should he start recording again.

Use your intercom to talk to all the students together at the beginning, and to tell them at the end that the class is over. Use it also to congratulate them if everything has gone well.

Whatever you do, don't be tolerant of inefficiency. Once a student gets into the habit of gabbling through exercises, without going back systematically, you will find it difficult to break him of the habit. The language laboratory, as a result, will merely consolidate his mistakes rather than help him.

Normally, you should have a laboratory assistant who will answer your cries for help.

10.12.6. Some basic questions

(a) How long should each session be?
If monitoring is good, the laboratory is very tiring. With efficient organisation, half an hour sessions should be enough.

(b) How many times should classes go into the laboratory?
This depends on whether the textbook in use has laboratory work as an integral part of it. It also depends on the length and intensity of the actual course. If a course is short, it's hardly worth using the laboratory at all, as by the time students have learnt how to use it effectively, the course will be over. Given that there are many other skills which have to be taught outside the laboratory, a reasonable proportion would seem to be about half an hour's lab work for every five hours' classes, and a quarter of an hour for preparation in class. However, a lot obviously depends on the teaching objectives and the students themselves. If there has to be a choice, the laboratory is probably better used for beginners rather than advanced students.

(c) Is a tape library necessary?
With a tape library, the teacher can put the tape that is needed in each booth before the students come into the laboratory. Otherwise, the master tape has to be played from the console and recorded on all the students' tapes before they start work.

A tape library involves extra cost as you need as many pre-recorded sets of exercises as there are students. However, the student can start work immediately he goes in. If, on the other hand, all the tapes are recorded while the students are in their booths, they can listen to the exercises before starting on them, which is also advantageous.

Considering costs, the advantages of a tape library would, therefore, seem to be minimal, particularly as the students have to wait while you put the tapes in their booths in any case. A library is, however, necessary for private study, where each student uses an individual tape.

Further reading

1   Byrne, D., *Teaching Oral English*, Longman, 1986. Chapter 12.

2   Holden, S., *Visual Aids for Oral Interaction*, MEP.

3   Jones, C., and Fortescue S., *Using Computers in the Language Classroom*, Longman, 1987.

Discussion

1   Why is it important to use visual aids? Are there any dangers attached to their use?

2   Discuss the advantages and disadvantages of using a language laboratory in language teaching. Compare its usefulness with that of a tape recorder in the classroom.

3   What resources/equipment do you think it is *essential* to have available, and which items are luxury extras?

Exercises

1   Make some flash cards that would be useful for the teaching of sounds. Describe how you would use them in class.

2   Choose a wall chart and say how you would use it:
      (a) to provide prompts in a substitution drill;
      (b) to practise dialogues;
      (c) to stimulate discussion.

3   Choose some pictures to be used for oral composition and describe the stages you would go through in class, stating what language items you would concentrate on.

4   Devise a laboratory exercise to practise enjoy + gerund, e.g. 'I enjoy swimming.'

11 Reading and writing practice

If the classroom is used mainly for aural/oral work there is an obvious need for reading and writing. This is often best done as homework, to consolidate what has been done orally. Reading and writing also need to be practised as skills in themselves.

11.1. Reading

A distinction needs to be made between intensive reading, where the student is expected to read short passages and understand everything, and extensive reading where the student reads to understand the main idea of a passage, but is not concerned with understanding every word.

Reading passages can be used for intensive study in class, for introducing and consolidating structure and vocabulary, as a springboard for other classroom activities, to increase pupils' passive vocabulary and for pleasure.

Texts used in class should preferably be short. As with all classroom activities, you need to ask yourself why you are using it. Do you want to increase vocabulary? Do you want to train students to answer questions precisely about a passage they can understand – in which case the passage should not be too difficult? Is the context of the passage important to your students? In other words, if they are technicians, or business men, or students of literature, does it tell them something useful and relevant? Can you combine the exercise with précis, and ultimately some kind of composition? Or do you want the class to prepare the passage at home as a basis for oral analysis next day? Or do you want, somehow, to combine all these things?

If reading is set for homework, it is most effective if you check on it in class. It serves two principal purposes:

A: The acquisition of new passive vocabulary and idiom.

B: Accustoming students to read fast and with pleasure in English, while they absorb new language forms, as they go along.

If your aim is the acquisition of vocabulary and idiom, train your students to use a dictionary effectively. Be careful, though, not to set too difficult a text so that they get weighted down by new words.

If your aim is to get your students to read fast with pleasure then give them a reader which is easy. Tell them *not* to look up a word unless the sense of a passage is unclear, but to concentrate on the story, the characters and the description of places. Then devote part of your class to asking them questions. By these means, encourage them to read as much English as possible, whether newspapers, stories, or novels.

Don't confuse literary and language aims here. If your aim is linguistic don't insist that everything has literary value. Students will only read a lot if they are interested, whether in comics, detective stories or thrillers, so give them books they don't want to put down. If they are studying English literature, prepare their set books and try to generate enthusiasm before they start reading.

Every class should, preferably, have a reader at their level. There are many readers on the market and a sample list can be found at the end of this book.[1]

11.2 Writing

The main problem here is to get your students used to English ways of expressing themsleves. Thus, Spanish or Italian students tend to write long flowery sentences with an emphasis on resonance and style rather than context. The French have problems with paragraphs. With Arab or Iranian students, make sure they write clearly. The question of teaching Arabs and Iranians to form Latin script, however, is beyond the scope of this book. Get your students accustomed to writing in short sentences, each ending with a full stop. The French and other nationalities will tend to bridge different sentences with a comma.

Later, teach them how to join sentences with conjunctions such as 'so that', 'while', 'then', etc. Make sure of spelling by getting them to write out mis-spelt words.

Try not to set any written work which is too difficult; otherwise your students will translate from their own languages, and habits will grow which are difficult to eliminate. Make sure, therefore, that writing, except at advanced stages, consolidates what you have done in class.

Here, too, you must ask yourself what your students *need* to write: letters, narrative, reported speech, form-filling, description, note-taking. etc. Be meticulous about spelling and punctuation, and get them to copy out words they have mis-spelt.

11.3. Exercises

All textbooks have exercises – some good and some not so good. In general they are similar to oral exercises which have been outlined in this book: substitution, transformation, question and answer, etc. (see 4.3.). Many teachers are opposed to exercises which involve filling in blank words or changing the tense of a verb. However, these have a function as they make students aware of the way

1   See Appendix C.

language works. Preferably, though, they should be placed in a situation that is real, as with oral practice.

If you devise exercises, make them relevant to your students' needs. Relate them to pictures if you can. Make them follow patterns you have already done in class. Allow students to use their deductive powers. To take simple examples: if you want them to be familiar with numbers, give them sums which produce the numbers you want them to write. If you want them to describe what people wear, get them to describe what students in class were wearing. If you are going over furniture with 'there is/there are', relate it to a natural environment: 'In a *sitting room* there are armchairs, small tables, a lamp, pictures on the walls. In a *dining room* there is a big table, chairs, etc.'

11.4. Guided composition

As students advance, train them to create their own narrative or descriptive pieces because they will need them for letters, reports, etc. Here again you have to limit them. The first essays in composition can therefore be simple sentences derived from single words: 'chair', 'teacher', 'table', etc. These may seem stunted and over simple. However, this is inevitable at beginners' stage: at least the sentences relate to some sort of reality.

Later, you produce the outline of a composition which students fill out. At the beginning, this may simply be the routine of 'getting up', while practising the habitual Present:

get up – seven o'clock – bathroom – take a shower – brush teeth – bedroom – dress – breakfast – half past seven – leave the house – eight o'clock.

Here at a more advanced stage, is an outline for a railway journey for students in Rome. Here they are practising the Past, but you use the Present in your guide, so that students can change the tense themselves. It is in the form of a letter as this kind of narrative is more likely to be used by students at this level.

Dear Jean,
    Thanks for letter – Glad you're well etc. Just been to Naples – leave house – nine o'clock – with father – taxi – Termini Station – buy tickets – platform six – get into a compartment – train leaves – a quarter to ten – look through window – suburbs – green countryside – mountains – ticket collector – read the newspaper – two American tourists in compartment – talk about America – they say – suitcase falls – arrive Naples – get out – say goodbye to Americans – Must finish now etc. – Best wishes.

As your class advances, you can extend the scope. In the above, for intance, initiative is allowed for what the Americans said, and what happened when the suitcase fell, and for beginning and ending the letter.

11.5. Free composition

Free composition is the equivalent of free conversation among the writing skills. As with conversation, it is essential to interest your students. Your object is to practise their English, not to challenge them to something difficult or unfamiliar. First, decide what secondary skills you want to practise. Is it description or narrative, or argument, or letter writing, or the ability to persuade? Are you trying to get them to express their personal feelings or general ideas? Or are you aiming to combine a number of these? Once you have decided, then give your students as varied a choice of subject as possible, and ask your class if they like any of them.

If they don't, write up more. Help, if necessary with ideas on how to deal with these themes.

You may also have to teach how to construct actual compositions. Apart from the French and Germans, most nationalities do not write compositions at school.

After the first compositions have been returned, take one of them, and go over it. Is there a beginning, a middle and an end? Are the ideas set out clearly, and contrasted? Are the paragraphs and stages of thought clear? If it is a descriptive piece, say of a student's home when he was a child, are the different areas of description clear? Or are things that have previously been forgotten added haphazardly at the end?

If necessary, encourage your students to plan out a composition and go over this in class. Taking the description of a home, how would it be divided up? Possibly:

1   Where it was.
2   The garden. Neighbouring houses and streets.
3   The entrance.
4   The sitting room.
5   The dining room.
6   The bedrooms.
7   Overall impression.

Make sure, too, that your students learn to answer the question or describe the title of the essay precisely. In the above, it might be tempting to write about what actually happened in this childhood home: who lived there, family events, etc. However, this would strictly be beyond a *description* of the building. Sad as it may be, insist that the student eliminates anything unasked for. This is particularly important for exams or writing reports where questions have to be answered precisely, and you are also training your students to think clearly and concisely in English.

11.6. Précis

This involves condensing a long passage into a short one, and is a valuable thought process in any language. It is particularly useful for advanced classes and for training business men to summarise essential facts in a report or memorandum. It also leads to discussion in class and the sharpening of language to express precise ideas.

When preparing it, get your students to read through the passage by themselves. Then ask them what the first essential theme is. Write the best suggestion on the board, and rearrange it to make it as brief as possible. Then extract the remaining essentials. Then get the class to do the précis for homework. When they have become accustomed to the process, set them other passages without preparation, but you can go over them in the same way when you have collected and corrected them.

11.7. Correction

There is little point in your students working away if they are not going to learn as much as possible from any mistakes they make. The 'reward' for doing written work is the feeling that something is being learnt. If students sense that their teacher is too indifferent to correct efficiently, they follow his example and become reluctant to do any written work.

Some teachers do not like giving marks as it reminds them of miserably competitive schooldays. However, in my experience, students prefer clear assessment and there is no need to use this invidiously. With compositions, the most comprehensive method of correcting which I have found, was suggested by H. A. Cartledge. Here, you divide up mistakes into categories and use abbreviations in the margin to indicate them. Grammar: G; Spelling: SP; Word Order: WO; Punctuation: P; Vocabulary: V; Prepositions: PR; Verb: VB.

You underline mistakes so that the student can still see what he originally wrote. At the end, you add up the errors under each category, and list them. The student can see where he is weakest, and as he does more compositions, he can – hopefully – note his improvements in particular areas of English. If the teacher wants to give marks, he starts from a total of, say, thirty. He awards a mark out of 10 for length, quality of composition and intangibles, and takes one mark off the remaining twenty for each mistake. If any of these mistakes are bad or careless, he takes two marks off.

In the interests of clarity, train students to write on every other line, which is useful also for their own corrections and a great advantage in exams.

From intermediate level on, you can plan much of your teaching round these mistakes. Before returning the written work, go through the compositions or exercises, one by one, and comment on mistakes which you think are common to most of the class, without of course saying whose homework you are looking at.

Remember to return written work as soon as possible. If you delay, interest will wane. At the same time, the fact that you return written work promptly shows that you care.

Here is an example:

HOME TOWN

We have no home town, say the people in Tokyo. Most people
in Tokyo came from the rural areas of Japan in order to find
their jobs or to study. They seem to have their home towns
in the places where they were brought up, but they usually
say that they have no home town. As it is difficult for them
to say that Tokyo is their home town, there is no place which
they can call their 'home town' in the place where they spent
their days in youth, let alone in Tokyo.

However, I think it is sure that they have their home town in
G their minds or in their dreams if you like. For some people the
forests which are surrounded by the mountains may be in their
minds. They may be still walking along the long, narrow roads
G to the forests in their dreams. For the other people, the
rivers where they used to swim, shrieking with excitement every
P hot summer day, may be in their dream. They might remember that
the water was shining in the sun. They may be still talking
                                    escapades
V to their naughty friends about their mischieves in the shade
under the big, tall oaks after swimming in their dreams

They might still hear their naughty friends talking to them.
G But these people know that all that they dream have gone away
G and they can't find them anywhere.

P Tokyo, where those who lost their home towns live, is more
terrible than strange. The people lead their lives as if they
S were seaweed which has lost its root. They have no place
G to go back. The place where they now live is nothing but the
S cave of the prehistoric people. Only a poet read a poem 'There
G is a place for me to back in the blue sky'. Still, it's almost
impossible for them to see the sky. Nowadays a lot of people
G begin to doubt as to where they come from and where they are going to.
G The people who lost their home towns are the people who had no
destination. Comment Poetic and well-expressed.
Style: too much repetition of 'home town' and 'dream'
N.B "To get back to" 'people haves
Mistakes   Punctuation 2   Vocabulary 1
            Grammar 8   Spelling 2
            $\frac{7}{20} + \frac{8}{10} = \boxed{\frac{15}{30}}$

Further reading

1 On reading:
   Rivers, Wilga, *Teaching Foreign Language Skills*, University of Chicago Press, 1980. Chapter 9, pp. 213-239.
2 On writing:
   Byrne, D., *English Teaching Perspectives*, Longman, 1980.
   Byrne, D., *Teaching Writing Skills* (New Edition), Longman, 1988.
3 On reading and writing:
   Finocchiaro, Mary, *Teaching English as a Second Language*, Harper and Row, 1969. Chapter 4, pp. 134-163.
   Nuttall, C., *Teaching Reading Skills in a Foreign Language*, Heinemann, 1982.

Discussion

1 Would you use essay writing with all pupils? When would it be a useful skill to practise?

2 How could you encourage your students to read extensively outside the classroom and how would you ensure that they do it?

Exercises

1 Devise a guided composition in the form of a letter for a class of Spanish teenagers learning English in Madrid.

2 Look at the composition on p. 122. How would you help this pupil eliminate his mistakes?

3 Choose a passage you could use for a précis and write out the stages you would go through in class.

12 Syllabus planning and lesson planning

Various teaching approaches have now been presented. By a process of experimentation each teacher will find the techniques that best suit him, his students, and the particular aspects of the language he is teaching. Try everything – even if it doesn't at first sight appeal to you.

Teaching over weeks, months, or years means integrating everything into a varied progression. Normally this is done with a textbook as guide and, possibly, as inspiration.

12.1. Evaluating a textbook

A textbook can only really be tested out in class. However, it would be impossible to try out all available textbooks in this way, and some kind of assessment has to be made.

WHY USE A TEXTBOOK?

It may well be better to use prepared material, or a series of textbooks brought into class to fulfil different purposes, particularly at higher levels. However, psychologically, a textbook is important to a student. It is something concrete that gives a measure of progress and achievement as lessons are completed, one by one, until finally the book is finished. In schools where students are enrolled at various levels, it is also a measure of standards.

Ideally, every textbook should be chosen for a particular group; it should differ, depending on whether adults or children are taught; it should meet the learning requirements of a class as precisely as possible. However, it is difficult to find a tailor-made textbook unless the teacher writes it as he goes along.

One difficulty is that teachers often have different views from their students on the general appeal and interest of a textbook. However, it is particularly important that the teacher does not show open disapproval of a book. Students tend to like a textbook if the teacher is enthusiastic, and therefore, learn with more interest. However, if their teacher is ostensibly critical, they doubt the book's value and thus the value of the class itself.

SOME GENERAL CONSIDERATIONS

1 How long is your course? For example, a textbook chosen for a four week summer course probably needs to be different from one chosen for an academic year.

126

2 Who is the book for? Business men? Secondary school children? Which nationality?

3 How many hours do you teach a class per week? Courses of three hours a week may need different material from intensive courses.

4 Is the structural grading in the book appropriate? Will the students be taught what they want to know in the right order, with the right priorities?

5 Is the vocabulary useful and in current use? Is it too childish for adults or too adult for children? Is there too much of it?

6 Are the students taught the kind of idiomatic English they need, early enough? Are they, for instance, introduced to useful phrases, like 'How are you?', 'Can I have ...?', etc. at the beginning.

7 Will the reading passages, or the story line, interest the students?

8 Are the dialogues realistic and relevant and lively?

9 Is the book visually alive and well presented?

STUDENT'S POINT OF VIEW

1 Cost? If the student is paying for the book, is it within his means?

2 Is there plenty of scope for him to work on his own? Is there enough homework? Accompanying cassettes?

3 Are there too many cultural, or political barriers?

4 Will the book make students feel they are working with an up-to-date, convincing method?

5 Does the book give opportunities for student identification and personal expression, or will the learner just have to go along with what is presented to him?

6 Is the book so long that it never seems to come to an end?

7 Do all the lessons follow the same plan so that the student always knows what to expect?

TEACHER'S POINT OF VIEW

1 Will the book help to produce good, lively teaching plans?

2 Does it conform to your own teaching approach?

3 Can additional material be used effectively, or is there sufficient already?

4 Will it stimulate you to use the techniques you feel are necessary?

5 Will teaching parts of it embarrass, inhibit, or limit you?

6 Will it allow you to get the necessary speed and tempo, or will it drag you down? Do you feel parts of it are bound to make your lessons boring?

7 Does it bring out all the secondary skills you want to teach your students?

8 Is each lesson the right length so that it fits in well with the timetable?

With more advanced classes, a basic textbook is often advisable. Here the ideal is a textbook which meets the above requirements, but which does not impose itself too much, so that additional material can be used.

12.2. Using a textbook

Having evaluated various textbooks and chosen one that seems suitable, you

still have to look carefully at how you are going to use it. Even a textbook written
for one nationality and age group cannot fit the needs and interests of every class
precisely. You have, therefore, to interpret both ideas and material.

First, examine the general outline and the lessons which are at the level of your
class. Look at the introduction to the teacher's book: What are the author's
teaching ideas? What techniques does he recommend? What about homework?
Then go over the students' book in parallel with the teacher's book. Look at the
development of lessons and decide if you want to change anything because of the
particular requirements of your class.

When you have done this, work out what you hope to accomplish in the first
ten or fifteen hours. Then write the plan of your first two lessons in detail.

12.3. Adapting to a class

You want to know as much about your students as possible. One way initially
is to duplicate a questionnaire such as the following in your students' language.

Name ....

Address ....

....

How many brothers? ....

How many sisters? ....

Have you ever been abroad? ....

Which countries and how long? ....

....

Do you speak any other languages? ....

Where have you lived and how long? ....

....

What are your main interests? e.g. football, cinema, etc. ....

....

What profession do you want to follow? ....

What is your favourite school subject? ....

Why do you want to learn English? ....

....

With the answers you have some idea of background and motivation. You
can also use them in class. If someone wants to be an engineer, you concentrate
on him when introducing the word. If some students have travelled to countries
whose nationality comes up, you can turn to them first.

12.4. Intermediate classes

Here, planning can follow similar lines. As your students know more English,
there is more material available: there is more scope for imagination when

creating situations; there is more room for using different approaches, whether chain stores, or mime, wall charts or composition. You can also use your students more, and get them to learn more by themselves by developing their ingenuity and powers of deduction. It is just as important to teach relevant structure and ways of communicating, as at the beginners' stage. At the same time, it is more tempting to teach irrelevant language, and thus to lose tempo.

There is also the question of revision. An intermediate class often makes beginners' mistakes. If you revise at length, there is less sense of progress. Classes should, therefore, be a blend of presentation, consolidation and remedial teaching. You have to hold a large number of different threads, and weave them into a colourful pattern as you go along.

Intermediate textbooks usually contain a mass of material, which, when plodded through, slows progression. You need, therefore, to be able to decide what to introduce rapidly, what to revise later, what to get your students to do at home, and what to examine in depth.

At this stage, too, you want your students to learn particular ways of expressing themselves in English which depend on mood and attitude. You need to integrate these with your pronunciation and structure teaching.

12.5. Advanced stages

It is difficult to find a textbook which covers the different learning angles which an advanced class needs. However, a book of dialogues or structure practice, or a novel or play, can provide an anchor.

Before taking an advanced class, familiarise yourself with any extra material needed. Make sure that your syllabus is sufficiently varied. Base it on what your students are trying to attain, whether it is passing an exam, English for special purposes, or a general consolidation of useful aspects of language.

Among the latter, we could list the following:

Fluency of expression in speaking and writing – Ability to understand different forms of English, whether spoken by Americans, Australians, Scotsmen, etc. or on the radio, in films, etc. – Increase of relevant vocabulary – Revision and perfecting of structural usage – Ability to understand and express different moods and attitudes, e.g. persuasion, polite refusals, requests, etc. – Use and understanding of relevant idioms – Ability to read newspapers, dialogue, novels, plays, etc. – Ability to discuss and argue – Increase in general knowledge of the English speaking world.

Here is an example of a week's syllabus for a general English course for fifteen students at this level:

	Monday	Tuesday	Wednesday	Thursday	Friday
9.00	Give back homework.	Give back homework.	Give back homework.	Give back homework.	Give back homework.
9.15	Précis.	Comprehension passage.	Dictation.	Going over compositions.	Idiomatic English.
10.00	Taped dialogue. Comprehension and acting out.	Wall Chart. Ext. of vocab. Descriptions.	Pron. Exercises.	Discussing project.	Newspapers. Vocab. style, discussion.
11.00	Background to Britain/America, etc.	Project.	Discuss Reader.	Moods and attitudes.	Prepared discussion.
Home-work.	Short précis.	Question and answer on comprehension passage.	Writing up project.	Writing a dialogue. Prepare discussion theme.	Composition.
Reading a short story, play or novel.					

As it is an advantage to hear as many different people speaking English as possible, it might be advisable to have several teachers fitting into this timetable. Notice the need for a good supply of tapes, wall charts, readers, newspapers, and précis and comprehension passages.

As advanced students easily grow impatient and normally think they know more than they do, a fast tempo would probably be necessary and a variety of techniques would need to be used. What you are really doing when you divide up a syllabus in this way is to stress a number of immediate objectives. This kind of syllabus could change from week to week. It can also be adapted to particular needs.

Let us now take a group of five Japanese business men, who can write and read English easily, but who have difficulty understanding or producing spoken English. They come to class for two hours, three days a week.

As there are only five students, half an hour is allotted to each activity, and as the students are Japanese, they will be familiar with cassettes. As the students are businessmen, some of the material has a business content, and the wall charts and dialogues should be slanted that way.

Although reading aloud is of little value, per se, it is used here to make the students more aware of the contrast between written and spoken English.

With these suggestions for integrating learning skills, techniques, aids and objectives into a teaching plan, try working out your own. Don't imitate the plan on p 131 precisely, as plans vary with the teaching situation. Adapt the general ideas to your class and to your own personality, within the bounds of common sense.

	Monday	Wednesday	Friday
9.00	Quick questions.	Discussion of cassette dialogue.	Discussion on report.
9.15	Wall chart: Vocabulary and description.	Prepared discussion.	Oral précis of report.
10.00	Pronunciation exercises.	Reading aloud. Dictation.	Social English.
10.30	Cassette dialogue. Comprehension.	Taped prose passage. Question and answer.	Discussing newspaper.
Homework	Familiarisation of cassette dialogue. Preparation of discussion.	Reading a business report. Reading a newspaper.	Seeing a particular film, or television programme in English.

Discussion

1 How would you examine a textbook in detail before making out a syllabus and lesson plans?

2 What material would you want in a textbook for advanced classes? What other material would you bring into class?

3 How would you get to know your students during your first lesson with them?

Exercises

1 Take any textbook for beginners and assess it by the criteria outlined in this chapter.

2 List what you would want a complete lesson in a textbook for intermediate students to contain.

3 Take any textbook and make out a syllabus you might follow for five lessons with a group of 15 French students in France.

4 Make out a timetable for an advanced class consisting of 10 Italians in the hotel business whose speech is fluent but often grammatically incorrect; their ability to read and write is a long way behind their oral expression. They are studying three hours a day for ten working days.

Appendix A EFL exams

All these exams can be held both in the U.K. and in other countries.

Trinity College – Oral exam
Held by each school according to demand. The school decides the date and Trinity provide the Examiners, normally with three weeks' notice. There are 12 grades, ranging from Beginners (Grade 1) to Post-Proficiency (Grade 12). Psychologically, a good exam which students enjoy.

Trinity College of Music,
11 Mandeville Place,
London W1M 6AQ
01 935 5773

ARELS certificate – Oral exam in laboratory
This is taken in a language laboratory and lasts an hour. It is designed for Post-Intermediate students and is invaluable as a test of expression and knowledge of spoken English. Held in mid-May, August and November for which the closing dates are 3/4 weeks in advance.

ARELS,
125 High Holborn
London WC1V 6QD
01 242 3136

ARELS diploma
This follows the same format as the Certificate but is at a much higher level (Proficiency). Many students find this a difficult and challenging exam. It is only held in mid-May and November, according to demand. Address as for Certificate.

Oxford exam
This is at preliminary and higher levels and consists of reading and writing tests. It is often held in conjunction with the ARELS exams (see above) but can also be taken separately. March and November.

Cambridge Preliminary test
This is at the elementary/early intermediate level. It consists of an interview of about seven minutes and a listening test lasting half an hour, as well as a written exam paper.

Cambridge First Certificate

This comprises a written section lasting $5\frac{1}{4}$ hours and an oral exam of approximately 40 minutes, including an interview and a listening comprehension. The written part includes a composition paper, a reading comprehension and English open-completion tests. The exam is held in mid-June and mid-December.

Syndicate Buildings,
17 Harvey Road,
Cambridge CB1 2EV
Cambridge 61111

Closing date for June is at the end of March and for December is early October.

Cambridge Proficiency

This follows the same format as First Certificate but at a *much* higher level. Students are advised to allow a year after taking First Certificate before they go on to Proficiency. Times and closing dates and address is the same as for First Certificate.

The R.S.A. exams

There are in the communicative use of English as a foreign language. There are separate exams in reading, writing, listening and oral interaction at three levels, and students can select from them according to their needs. Exams are held twice a year in May and November.

R.S.A. Publications Ltd.,
Murray Road,
Orpington, Kent BR5 4RB
Orpington 32421

Appendix B Structure list

The following grading can be varied according to students' needs.

Beginners

1 To be
   - Affirmative.
   - Interrogative.
   - Negative.
   - Q. tag.

   also question words: Who? What? Where? Why?
2 Indefinite article with occupations: I'm *a* doctor.
3 This/that, these/those.
4 Singular and plural nouns, regulars + irregulars.
5 Imperative and negative imperative.
6 Adjectives and word order.
7 Present Continuous: He's playing.
8 To have (got).
9 (a) Possessive adjectives, e.g. It's my book.
   (b) 'Whose?'
10 Possessive pronouns.
11 Genitive with people (sing. and pl.), e.g. It's Susan's. The Browns'.
   with things, e.g. The back of the car.
12 Present Simple: He works, etc.
13 Frequency adverbs: often, never, sometimes, always, etc.
14 There is/there are.
15 There's a/it's a.
16 Some/any/q. and neg.
17 Simple prepositions.
18 I can.
19 The time.
20 Was/were.
21 Simple Past tense.
22 Simple Past tense in irregular verbs.
23 The weather (a) as adjectives: It's cloudy, rainy, fine, etc.
              (b) as Pres. Cont/Pres. Simp. contrast:
                  It's raining/It rains a lot.
24 Future with 'going to'.
25 Adverb formation + -ly.
26 Adverb order (manner, place or time)

He works $\begin{cases} \text{hard.} \\ \text{at home.} \\ \text{every evening.} \end{cases}$

27 A lot/much/many.
28 A little/few.
29 Future + will + negative.
30 Questions + *shall* we.
31 More complicated frequency adverbs + revision Pres. Simple, e.g. hardly ever, nearly, always, etc.
32 Past Continuous
       contrast: Past Simple + while
       While he was *writing*, the door *opened*.
33 1st (open) Conditional: if it rains we'll go to the cinema.

Elementary
34 Present Perfect + 'just'.
35 Present Perfect + for ⎫
36 Present Perfect + since ⎬ – simple and continuous.
37 Present Perfect contrasted with Past Simple: I've been there/I was there yesterday.
38 Present Perfect + 'already'.
39 Present Perfect Qn + 'yet'.
40 Too/enough.
41 Simple (short-word) comparatives.
42 Long-word comparatives + 'more'.
43 Simple superlatives.
44 Long-word superlatives + 'most' + in . . .
                           + of the three etc.
45 Relatives . . . who (subject)
               that (subject)
               ommission (object), after 'the one', 'the ones'.
46 Used to e.g. Did you use to? I never used to.
47 Must/mustn't.
48 Must/needn't.
49 As . . . as + adjectives.
50 As . . . as = adverbs.
51 The same . . . as.
52 Can/will be able to.
53 Want to . . .
54 Want + Acc. + to.
55 Prepositions with time.
56 Reported commands, e.g. He told me to . . .
57 Reported commands in negative, e.g. He told me not to . . .
58 Must/will have to.
59 Must/had to.
60 May, permission and possibility.

61 Phrasal verbs (simple) + word order in pronouns.
62 Present Continuous for Future.
63 Although.
64 Infinitive of purpose.
65 So that.
66 For + gerund.
67 Unless + 1st Conditional.
68 Temporal conjunctions (a) Present simple – When I go . . .
                             (b) Present Perfect – When I've been . . .
69 Need + gerund.

Intermediate

70 2nd Conditional: If I went to Russia, I'd visit Moscow.
71 Adjective and infinitive: It's pleasant to live in the country.
72 Reported speech – Future to Conditional.
                     Present to Past, etc.
73 Reported questions (a) with Qn. words.
                        (b) with if/whether.
74 Adjective phrases + participle, e.g. A man carrying a gun . . .
75 Noun clauses, e.g. I don't know what to do/how to say it, etc.
76 Passive – all simple tenses.
            – all continuous (+ being) tenses.
77 Passive Infinitive + can, must, should, need to, etc.
78 He must be a policeman (log. conclusion).
79 Think, hope, suppose, expect + so.
80 Should ⎫
    Or   ⎬ for obligation.
81 Ought ⎭
82 Use of 'the' (a) abstracts
                  (b) plurals
                  (c) uncountables
                  (d) meals
                  (e) countries
                  (f) hospital/prison/bed, etc after prepositions.
83 Reflexive verbs.
84 Past Perfect (a) after certain conjunctions,
                       e.g. after, before, because, as soon as.
85   (b) following 'realised', 'remembered', 'visited'.
86 Past Perfect Continuous.
87 Verbs + gerund, e.g. finish/enjoy, etc.
88 Verbs + infinitive (+ to).
89 Verbs + prep. + gerund.
90 Future Continuous.
91 Say/tell.
92 Difference between so + adjectives and such + noun.
93 Have + do (habit), e.g. *I don't have lunch.*

94 Inversion ... *SO* (a) *can I.*
                        (b) *do I.*
95 Inversion ... *Neither* do I.
96 Future Perfect Simple.
97 Future Perfect Continuous.
98 Word order + adverb phrases (manner, place, time).

Advanced

 99 Be/get used to + gerund in various tenses.
100 Uses of either/neither.
101 Make (= construct).
102 Do (activity).
103 Suggest (+ subjunctive) in Present + Past.
104 $\left\{\begin{array}{l}\text{I meant to} \dots \text{(but)} \dots \\ \text{I was going to} \dots \end{array}\right.$
105 (a) $\left\{\begin{array}{l}\text{am} \\ \text{was}\end{array}\right\}$ $\left\{\begin{array}{l}\text{meant} \\ \text{supposed}\end{array}\right\}$ to ...
     (b)
106 Let + object + verb.
107 Make + object + verb. (Contrast : be made to do).
108 (a) I wish $\left.\begin{array}{l}\\\\\end{array}\right\}$ + seq. of tenses.
     (b) If only
109 3rd Conditional.
110 Remember + ing $\left.\begin{array}{l}\\\\\end{array}\right\}$
                    + to   see 87/88
111 Try   + ing $\left.\begin{array}{l}\\\\\end{array}\right\}$
                + to
112 Stop   + ing $\left.\begin{array}{l}\\\\\end{array}\right\}$ see 87/88
                + to
113 He must have gone out.
114 He must have been going out.
115 He can't have $\left\{\begin{array}{l}\text{gone.} \\ \text{been going out.}\end{array}\right.$
116 He might have $\left\{\begin{array}{l}\text{gone.} \\ \text{been going out.}\end{array}\right.$
117 (a) needn't have, (b) didn't need to.
118 Surely/certainly.
119 Fairly/rather.
120 It's $\left\{\begin{array}{l}\text{high} \\ \text{about}\end{array}\right\}$ time we *left*.
121 I'd rather you *took* (my old umbrella).
122 I saw a man cross/crossing the road.

Appendix C Reading for enjoyment (sample list[1])

Beginners

Detectives from Scotland Yard	– Longman Structural Readers Stage 1 – L.G. Alexander
The Flying Spy	– Longman Structural Readers Stage 1 – Alwyn Cox
The Prisoners	– Longman Structural Readers Stage 1 – D. Byrne
King Henry	– Longman Structural Readers Stage 1
The Car Thieves	– Longman Structural Readers Stage 1 – L. G. Alexander
Operation Janus	– Longman Structural Readers Stage 1 – L. G. Alexander
The Battle of Newton Road	– Longman Structural Readers Stage 1 – L. Dunkling

Mid Elementary

K's First Case	– Longman Structural Readers Stage 2 – L. G. Alexander
The Swiss Family Robinson	– O.U.P.
Nasreddin	– O.U.P.
April Fools' Day	– Longman Structural Readers Stage 2 – L. G. Alexander

Elementary/Early Intermediate

The African Queen	– New Method Supplementary Readers Stage 4 – C. S. Forester
Operation Mastermind	– Longman Structural Readers Stage 3 – L. G. Alexander
In the Beginning	– Longman Structural Readers Stage 2 – John Christopher

[1] For a full reading list, contact the individual publishers concerned.

Mid Intermediate

The Thirty Nine Steps — Longman Structural Readers
Stage 4 – J. Buchan

The Forger — Longman Structural Readers
Stage 4 – Robert O'Neill

The Birds and Other Stories — Longman Structural Readers
Stage 4 – Daphne du Maurier

David and Marianne — Longman Structural Readers
Stage 3 – John Dent

The Man in the Train — University of London Press
E. F. Candlin

Dangerous Game — Longman Structural Readers
Stage 3 – William Harris/L G
Alexander

Late Intermediate

The Last Post — Collier Macmillan
Alan R. Beesley

The Smuggler — Heinemann Educational Books
Piers Plowright

The Kon-Tiki Expedition — Longman Structural Readers
Stage 6 – T. Heyerdahl

The Go-Between — Longman Structural Readers
Stage 6 – L. P. Hartley

The Midwich Cuckoos — New Method Supplementary Readers
Stage 3 – J. Wyndham

Cider with Rosie — Longman Structural Readers
Stage 6–Laurie Lee

Intermediate/Advanced

The Triffids — Hutchinson Educational Books
J. Wyndham

Kiss Kiss — Penguin – R. Dahl

Three Men in a Boat — Longman Simplified English Series
Jerome K. Jerome

Moby Dick — Longman Simplified English Series
Herman Melville

The Drivers Seat — Macmillan – Muriel Spark

Advanced

The Daughter of Time — Penguin – J. Tey
The Franchise Affair — Penguin – J. Tey
The Sandcastle — Penguin – Iris Murdoch
Wordscapes — O.U.P. – Barry Maybury

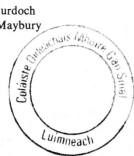